MW01032361

Ka Lei Ha'aheo

Ka Lei Ha‘aheo

Teacher's Guide and Answer Key

Alberta Pualani Hopkins

University of Hawaii Press

Honolulu

© 1992 University of Hawaii Press

All rights reserved

ISBN 0–8248–1372–3

Printed in the United States of America

01 02   8 7 6 5

University of Hawai'i Press books are printed
on acid-free paper and meet the guidelines
for permanence and durability of the Council
on Library Resources.

Contents

Contents

Format of Ka Lei Haʻaheo

I. THE TEXT

With the exception of Haʻawina 1 and 2, all the lessons in the text follow the same format. Each begins with Part I, Basic Sentences. These are examples of the grammatical patterns introduced in the lesson and vocabulary items of special interest.

Next comes Part II, Explanations. These cover the new constructions, special vocabulary, and relevant cultural concepts.

Part III, Dialogs, is based partly on the new grammatical constructions and vocabulary, but also draw extensively on previously introduced material. Most of the conversations concern one Hawaiian family or college classroom and dormitory situation and utilize common everyday subjects and expressions. The dialogs are followed by a brief discussion of some of the Hawaiian cultural values and practices they illustrate.

Part IV, Exercises, includes practice for material introduced in the lesson and also reviews of previous lessons.

Part V, Vocabulary, lists the new words, idioms, and common phrases used in the lesson.

The material in each lesson in the text has been arranged in logical sequence for a student who is reviewing after classroom work, or for someone who is attempting to teach himself or herself. **It is NOT intended that the material should be taught in the order in which it is presented in each lesson.** Instead, the teacher should consult this Teacher's Guide for the general lesson plan.

The sequence of grammatical patterns in the lessons is ordered so that every three lessons can be grouped into a larger unit if the teacher so desires. Thus, Lessons 1–3, 4–6, 7–9, 10–12, 13–15, 16–18, 19–21, and 22–24 can be taught together. Following Lessons 6, 9, 12, 15, 18, 21, and 24 there are brief reviews *(hoʻi hope)* of the three preceding lessons. (Ho'i Hope 'Ekahi comes after the first six lessons.) Each review contains a list of the grammatical patterns and other points covered in the lessons and some practice material focusing on those areas.

The text is designed so that the first twelve lessons can be taught in one college semester of approximately sixteen weeks if the class meets daily. Hence, in addition to Hawaiian-English and English-Hawaiian vocabulary lists for the entire text, the book also has a Hawaiian-English vocabulary list for Lessons 1–12. This is intended to facilitate review at the end of the first semester and also to provide students who are beginning at Lesson 13 with the vocabulary that has already been introduced. The lists of idioms and phrases have been treated in the same way.

II. TEACHER'S GUIDE AND ANSWER KEY

This guide begins with a General Lesson Plan that outlines the order in which a lesson might be presented and offers some suggestions for using the material in the text and some personal pedagogical hints.

The General Lesson Plan is followed by the answer keys for the lessons and reviews. Each answer key after Lesson 1 begins with a list of the topics that are covered in the lesson. This is followed by a list of the "targets" in each basic sentence, then translations of the dialogs, and answers to the exercises. All of the possible correct answers to the exercises are not included. The answers provided are generally the forms that utilize the patterns introduced in the lesson.

General Lesson Plan

It is not intended that the material in *Ka Lei Ha'aheo* should be taught in the order in which it is presented in each lesson. For classroom use, I suggest following the general order described below.

I. VOCABULARY

In beginning a new lesson, the least threatening material for students is usually new vocabulary. Starting with this creates a comfortable and secure learning atmosphere.

There are many ways to introduce new words. Here are a few suggestions:

1. Use Pictures and Objects

Collect large pictures that you can show the entire class and smaller ones to paste on 5 × 8 cards for small group use. Draw your own; students especially enjoy your drawings if, like mine, they are not very good! Burningham, *Hawaiian Word Book,* (1983), is a good source, as are foreign language texts and teaching materials. Encourage students to bring pictures and objects that can be used in classroom drills.

2. Demonstrate the Meaning with Facial Expressions, Gestures and Actions

This obviously works best with verbs. Students enjoy guessing the meanings you are acting out.

3. Integrate the New Words into the Previous Lesson

Once students get familiar with the patterns in a lesson, they begin to get bored and lose interest; the attitude becomes, "We know this already." At this point, using new vocabulary from the next lesson in the "old" patterns provides a new challenge to the students.

With all these techniques, always give the class a chance to provide the target word before you supply it to them. And of course, have them look at you and not the text!

Often you will find that demonstrating the vocabulary leads naturally into the new grammatical constructions. In those instances, continue teaching the new patterns and do a systematic review of Part V, Vocabulary, later on. At other times it may be more convenient at this point to have students look at the vocabulary section with you. This is the time to point out glottal stops and macrons, similarities to other words they know, and other possible pitfalls in spelling and pronunciation. This is also a good place to discuss Hawaiian cultural concepts and values attached to various words. Remind students that the English glosses are only approximations of the meaning of the Hawaiian words, and that the Hawaiian words cannot always be used in the same contexts as the English "definitions."

I have found it useful to give a short quiz on new vocabulary two periods after it has been introduced; this encourages students to learn the vocabulary at the beginning of a new lesson rather than at the last minute.

II. EXPLANATIONS OF GRAMMATICAL CONSTRUCTIONS

After students are familiar with the new vocabulary, use it in teaching the grammatical patterns that are targeted in the lesson. It is almost always possible to introduce these patterns by demonstrating their meanings. Give grammatical explanations only after you have demonstrated a new pattern and students have grasped its meaning (you can see by their expressions when this happens!). Try to concentrate on **how** rather than **why.** Use the explanations in the book as a guide, expanding in your own words and providing more examples. Next give your students opportunities to practice the new pattern. Finally, after (1) Demonstration, (2) Explanation, and (3) Practice has been done with all the patterns, look at Part I, Basic Sentences, with your students as a (4) Review of the constructions and special vocabulary. The answer key for each lesson explains the target of each basic sentence.

You may find there are too many patterns to teach in one period. After teaching a pattern, assign the relevant exercises from Part IV of the lesson.

III. EXERCISES

A limited number of exercises has been provided in each lesson. Answers are available in the answer keys that are included in this guide, but keep in mind that there are often a number of correct answers to an exercise and all possibilities have not been included. Generally the exercises should be assigned as homework; they can be corrected in class orally or students can be asked to write them on the board, and the entire class can participate in identifying and correcting errors. Students can also be required to purchase the *Teacher's Guide and Answer Key* and to take responsibility for checking their answers and getting help from the teacher when necessary.

Other sources of exercises are the Department of Education, State of Hawaii, *Hawaiian Language Workbook* (1980) and *Lau Kukui* (1981).

IV. DIALOGS

After students have been introduced to the vocabulary and grammatical patterns and have started practicing by doing the exercises at home, they are ready to apply what they know to everyday situations by learning the dialogs. The more emphasis and time you can give to the conversations, the more proficient your class will become in listening and speaking skills, which have usually been the weakest points in Hawaiian language classes. The dialogs are intended to duplicate real-life situations and reflect Hawaiian values and styles of communication. They build on each other from lesson to lesson and contain material students can use outside of the dialogs with very few changes. The answer keys include translations of all the dialogs in each lesson.

Here is one sequence to use with a dialog:

1. Read through it once in Hawaiian; have the class mimic you.
2. Read it again; ask the students what each phrase means. Help them when they get stuck. Explain cultural values and styles reflected in the dialog.
3. Now practice the dialog in various ways with the whole class:
   a. You take one part; the class takes the other.
   b. Half the class takes one part; the other half takes the other part.
   c. Males take one part; females take the other.

Remember to switch parts so that everyone gets a chance to practice the whole dialog. After a couple of times, encourage students to rely on their memories to recite the dialogs; set the example yourself.

4. Finally, divide the class into pairs to practice. Circulate among them and model intonation, pronunciation, and so forth. **Do not criticize "mistakes."** Simply provide a model and have them imitate you.

5. Occasionally, ask three or four pairs to perform the dialog for the class and have the class judge the performances. Give lots of prizes.

V. FISH

This game, which is introduced in Lesson 4, is useful for practicing all kinds of patterns and enables students to speak Hawaiian in a natural situation. Because it happens early in their exposure to the language, it is psychologically rewarding and boosts their morale.

Use children's "Fish" cards; the ones I use have the fish pictures listed in Lesson 4. I just re-label them with the Hawaiian names. If you can't find "Fish" cards, you can use a regular deck of cards with Hawaiian fish name labels, or you can use the Hawaiian numbers and names for the jack *(keaka)*, queen *(wahine* or *mōʻī wahine)*, king *(kini* or *mōʻī)*, and ace *(ʻeka)*. Some teachers like to use colors as the names for the cards.

Three or four students play together. Each is dealt five cards, and the rest of the cards are placed face down and spread out in the "fish pond." Players take turns asking others for cards matching those in their hands. There should be four of each kind. If the person who is asked has the card, the person hands it over and the original player keeps asking. When the one who is asked doesn't have the right card, the person tells the player to take a dive. The player picks up a card from the pond; if the player gets what is wanted, he or she says *"Loaʻa"* and continues. If the player doesn't get it, it becomes the next person's turn. When a player has four of a kind, the player puts the matching cards face down on the table; that gives him or her a point. The player with the most points wins. If a player runs out of cards while there are still some in the pond, he or she picks up two more and continues playing. All of this sounds more complicated than it is; most classes have a number of students who have played this game as children.

This game can be used over and over again using different patterns for making the requests, such as *"He X kāu?"* or *"ʻEhia āu X?"* or *"Makemake au i kāu X."*

VI. TESTING

Giving a quiz after each lesson has been completely covered is very effective. It provides an incentive for students to do a thorough review before the next lesson begins. Because each lesson only contains one or two new patterns, the reviewing doesn't take too long and the quizzes can be short and easy to correct. After every three lessons, I give a longer test on a larger block of material that is interrelated. You will find a review *(hoʻi hope)* in the text following each set of interrelated lessons.

VII. JOURNALS

After students have studied Haʻawina 2, I ask them to keep a "journal." Every day they turn in a 4 × 6 card on which they have written at least one Hawaiian sentence, preferably about themselves and their experiences. The objective is to give them daily practice in writing Hawaiian and to give me an idea of where they are having grammatical problems. I correct these cards but do not grade them, and return them promptly. I keep track of the number turned in and give credit when computing the course grade. This is one fair way of giving credit to students who are conscientious and try hard but are not always "correct."

Students continually surprise me with how creative and funny they can be with these cards. Often they draw illustrations, write cartoons, or use the Sunday comics with their own captions. Most of them make use of the latest patterns they have learned. Sometimes I get serials and soap operas. Some students are also very open about sharing information about themselves. It can be a way for you to establish a personal relationship with students who want to do this. It gives you daily individual contact with each student. Often I find myself writing replies, and then there is the reward for the student of carrying on a correspondence in Hawaiian in a "real" situation.

This activity gives me valuable feedback from students on a number of levels and much personal satisfaction and pleasure. It can be used from the very beginning through all levels of skills classes. It provides students who save their cards a dramatic record of the growth and development of their language skills in the course of the semester or year. I strongly recommend that you try it; the rewards are well worth the bookkeeping involved.

Answer Keys

1

HAʻAWINA ʻEKAHI

I. TOPICS

A. Orthography
B. Pronunciation and spelling
C. Place names
    (See maps on p. 2.)

II. ANSWERS

D.   1. University of Hawaii main campus = Mānoa
      2. Windward Community College = Kāneʻohe
      3. Honolulu Zoo = Kapiʻolani Park

E.   1. Pearl Harbor = Puʻuloa
      2. Punchbowl = Pūowaina
      3. Chinaman's Hat = Mokoliʻi
      4. Temple Valley = ʻĀhuimanu
      5. Diamond Head = Lēʻahi (Kaimana Hila)
      6. Salt Lake = Āliamanu
      7. St. Louis Heights = Waʻahila
      8. Sacred Falls = Kaliuwaʻa
      9. Rabbit Island = Mānana

Except for Kaimana Hila, none of these names are translations of the English.

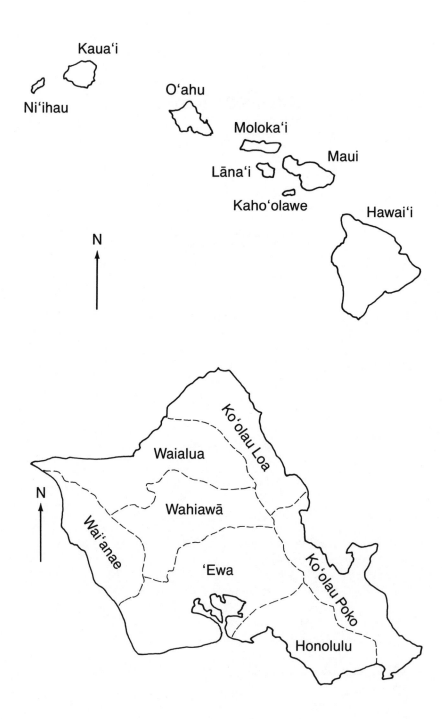

Kaua'i

Ni'ihau

O'ahu

Moloka'i

Lāna'i

Maui

Kaho'olawe

Hawai'i

N

Ko'olau Loa

Waialua

N

Wahiawā

Wai'anae

'Ewa

Ko'olau Poko

Honolulu

2

HAʻAWINA ʻELUA

I. TOPICS

A.   Class-inclusion sentences
 1. With modifiers
 2. With modifiers and adverbs
 3. With plural marker
 4. Question intonation pattern

B.   Demonstrative pronouns

C.   *Mau* plural marker

D.   *E* vocative

II. BASIC SENTENCE TARGETS

1. Class-inclusion sentence; *kēia*
2. Class-inclusion sentence; *kēnā*
3. Position of modifier
4. Position of plural
5. Question intonation (note that word order doesn't change); *kēlā*
6. *ʻAe;* note that question (sentence 5) and answer (sentence 6) have the same word order
7. Question intonation; *ʻoe*
8. Position of adverb; *au*
9. *E* vocative
10. *ʻAʻole*

III. ANSWERS

A.   1. he kanaka akamai
     2. he ʻīlio nui
     3. he kāne uʻi
     4. he pua nani
     5. he wahine pono

B.   1. E Lani, he aha kēlā?
     2. He moʻo kēlā.
     3. He ʻīlio kēnā?
     4. ʻAʻole, he pōpoki nui kēia.
     5. He mau pua nani loa kēia.
     6. He wahine uʻi loa ʻoe.
     7. He kanaka akamai kēia.
     8. He kāne pono kēlā?
     9. ʻAe, he kāne pono loa kēlā.
    10. E Waiwai, he kaʻa nui kēnā.

C.   1. That (near) is a pretty cat.
     2. You are a very mischievous woman.
     3. Nanea, that's a big car.
     4. I am a righteous person.
     5. Kalei, are you a very smart man?

D.   1. kēnā
     2. kēia
     3. ʻoe
     4. kēlā
     5. kēlā

3

HAʻAWINA ʻEKOLU

I. TOPICS

A. Equational sentences
B. *ʻO* nominative
C. Expanded class-inclusion sentences
D. *Ke/ka*
E. *Nō*
F. *Ia* (he, she, it)

II. BASIC SENTENCE TARGETS

1. Equational sentence; *ʻo wai* (with names, instead of *he aha*)
2. Answer to sentence 1; contrast of *kou/koʻu*
3. Equational sentence (identifying, introducing)
4. Equational sentence with common noun predicate; *ka*
5. Equational sentence with common noun predicate; *koʻu*
6. Equational sentence with noun phrase subject
7. Equational sentence; modifer + *loa* = superlative
8. Equational sentence with pronoun; reverse of English word order
9. Expanded class-inclusion sentence; noun phrase subject
10. Expanded class-inclusion sentence; proper noun subject

III. DIALOGS

1. Kanani and Kalei

Kanani:　Please, what's your name?
Kalei:　　My name is Kalei. Who are you?
Kanani:　Hi, Kalei. My name is Kanani.
Kalei:　　Hi, Kanani.
Kanani:　What's that?

Kalei: That's a big gecko. The gecko is a good thing.
Kanani: Thanks. Goodbye.
Kalei: Bye.

2. Pōhaku and Kalau

Pōhaku: Kalau, who's that?
Kalau: That's the Hawaiian language teacher.
Pōhaku: Is she a good teacher?
Kalau: Yes, she's a very good teacher.
Pōhaku: What's her name?
Kalau: Her name is Pua.
Pōhaku: Are you a Hawaiian language student?
Kalau: Yes, I'm a very happy student.
Pōhaku: Right, and you're a very nice boy. Thanks; goodbye.
Kalau: Goodbye.

IV. ANSWERS

A. 1. ke aloha nui
  2. ke kaikamahine pono
  3. ka iʻa ʻono
  4. ka pōpoki kolohe
  5. ke kumu kula

B. 1. ʻO kona kaʻa hou kēia?
  2. ʻO Hauʻoli kēlā keiki kāne momona.
  3. ʻO Momilani kona inoa.
  4. ʻO ʻoe ke kumu ʻōlelo Hawaiʻi?
  5. ʻO ka noho ʻoluʻolu loa kēnā.

C. 1. He haumana maikaʻi kēlā kaikamahine liʻiliʻi.
  2. He maiʻa ʻono ka maiʻa Pākē.
  3. He kanaka pono ʻo Kealiʻi.
  4. He wahine uʻi kēlā wahine momona.
  5. He keiki kāne kolohe kēia haumana hou.

D. 1. He haumana ʻōlelo Pākē ʻo ia?
  2. ʻO ia ke kumu ʻōlelo Pākē.
  3. ʻO Koko ka ʻīlio nui; ʻo Alā ka ʻīlio liʻiliʻi.
  4. He pōpoki ʻo ʻUmiʻumi.
  5. ʻO Leʻaleʻa ka mea kolohe.

E. 1. ka haumana akamai
    2. kēia haumana akamai
    3. He haumana akamai kēia.
    4. ʻO Kalei ka haumana akamai.
    5. ke keiki kāne wīwī
    6. kēlā keiki kāne wīwī
    7. He keiki kāne wīwī kēlā.
    8. ʻO Kimo kēlā keiki kāne wīwī.
    9. ka maiʻa Pākē
   10. kēnā maiʻa Pākē
   11. He maiʻa Pākē kēnā.
   12. He mea ʻono kēnā maiʻa Pākē.
   13. kēia pōpoki momona
   14. He pōpoki momona kēia.
   15. ʻO Garfield kēia pōpoki momona.

G. 1. Hoapili (close companion): the name given to Ulumaheihei by Kamehameha I when he chose him to hide his bones after his death (Pukui, *Hawaiian Folk Tales, Third Series,* 1933, p. 131).
    2. Kaleleokalani, Kaleleonālani: names for Queen Emma. After the death of their son, Kamehameha IV gave his wife a new name, Kaleleokalani, meaning "the flight of the chief." When Kamehameha IV died shortly thereafter, the queen changed her name to Kaleleonālani, meaning "the flight of the chiefs"; this was the name with which she signed her personal letters during the remainder of her life (Kuykendall, *The Hawaiian Kingdom,* 1953, vol. 2, pp. 280–281).
    3. Kamakaʻeha (the sore eyes): another name for Queen Liliʻuokalani, given at her birth by the regent Kinaʻu, who was suffering from sore eyes (Elbert and Mahoe, *Na Mele o Hawaiʻi Nei,* 1975, pp. 75–76).
    4. Paiʻea (hard-shelled crab): a name given to Kamehameha I by his defeated enemies in recognition of his impenetrable courage and endurance (Pukui et al., *Nana i ke Kumu,* 1972, vol. I, p. 97).

4

HAʻAWINA ʻEHĀ

I. TOPICS

A. Imperative sentences
B. Direct objects and markers *(i/iā)*
C. Indirect objects or destinations *(i/iā)*
D. Directionals

II. BASIC SENTENCE TARGETS

1. Imperative sentence; *aku;* direct object *(i)*
2. Imperative sentence; indirect object *(iā)*
3. Imperative sentence; no directional or subject; indirect object *(i)*
4. Imperative sentence; *mai;* no subject; *iaʻu*
5. Locational sentence *(eia)*
6. Imperative sentence; destination *(i)*
7. Imperative sentence; *iho*
8. Imperative sentence; *aʻe*
9. Imperative sentence; come *(hele mai)*
10. Imperative sentence; go *(hele aku)*

III. DIALOGS

1. The teacher and Kaleo

The teacher:	Hi, Kaleo.
Kaleo:	Hi, teacher.
The teacher:	What's that?
Kaleo:	That's my new car.

The teacher:	It's a really beautiful car. Please give me the key.
Kaleo:	Oh, wow! Here's the key. You take good care of my car.
The teacher:	Yes, (and) you take care of your body. See you later.
Kaleo:	Bye.

Later, at Kaleo's house:

Kaleo:	Hi, teacher.
The teacher:	Hi. Here's your car.
Kaleo:	Come, come, come and eat.
The teacher:	Thanks, Kaleo. This is a nice house.
Kaleo:	Sit down. Here's the poi and fish. Eat up!
The teacher:	This is really delicious fish. Please give me the salt.
Kaleo:	Here's the salt and here's the beer. Drink up!
The teacher:	Wow! You're really a good student. Thanks a lot.
Kaleo:	You're welcome. You're a good teacher. Goodbye.
The teacher:	Goodbye; take care of yourself.

IV. ANSWERS

A.
1. E hāʻawi aku ʻoe i kēnā penikala iā Kaʻolu!
2. E inu iho ʻoe i kēia pia!
3. E kiʻi aku ʻoe i kona kaʻa!
4. E mālama pono ʻoe iā ia!
5. E hoʻi mai ʻoe i ka hale!
6. E hele iho ʻoe i ke kai!
7. E hāʻawi aku ʻoe i kēia iʻa i ka pōpoki liʻiliʻi!
8. E ʻai iho ʻoe i kēia maiʻa Pākē ʻono!
9. E luʻu iho ʻoe!
10. E ʻōlelo Hawaiʻi mai ʻoe (iaʻu)! or E ʻōlelo mai ʻoe (iaʻu) i ka ʻōlelo Hawaiʻi! E ʻōlelo mai ʻoe i ka ʻōlelo Hawaiʻi (iaʻu)!

B.
1. *mai*
2. *aku*
3. *iho*
4. *aʻe*
5. *mai*

C.
1. *i*	6. *iā*
2. *iā*	7. *i*
3. *iā*	8. *iā*
4. *iā*	9. *iā*
5. ø	10. ø

D. 1. *e*
    2. *'o*
    3. *'o*
    4. *e*
    5. *'o*

E. 1. *ka*   6. *ka*
    2. *ke*   7. *ka*
    3. *ka*   8. *ka*
    4. *ke*   9. *ka*
    5. *ka*   10. *ke*

F. 1. E Kalani, e kū a'e 'oe!
    2. E ki'i aku 'oe i ka pia a me ka i'a.
    3. E hā'awi aku 'oe i ka i'a i ka pōpoki.
    4. E hā'awi mai 'oe i ka pia ia'u.
    5. E ho'i aku 'oe i kou noho.
    6. E noho iho 'oe.
    7. Mahalo, e Kalani. He haumana akamai loa 'oe.

G. 1. 'O wai kona inoa?
    2. E 'olu'olu 'oe, e ki'i aku 'oe i ka poi a me ka pa'akai.
    3. E hā'awi aku 'oe i kēia pua nani i kēlā wahine u'i.
    4. 'O ka lawai'a kēlā kanaka.
    5. 'O ka puke 'ōlelo Hawai'i kēia.
    6. He kāne hau'oli 'o ia.
    7. He i'a 'ono Ka 'ahi.
    8. He 'īlio nui 'o Koko.

The subject *'oe* may be omitted from the imperative sentences.

5

HAʻAWINA ʻELIMA

I. TOPICS

A. Personal pronouns
B. Stative verb sentences
C. *Nā*
D. Greetings
E. Divisions of the day

II. BASIC SENTENCE TARGETS

 1. Time greeting
 2. Pronoun greeting
 3. Time and pronoun greeting
 4. Stative question; pronoun subject
 5. Stative question; noun subject; *nā*
 6. Stative statement
 7. Stative statement; *ʻano; māua*
 8. Stative statement with adverb; *lākou*
 9. Stative statement; noun subject
10. Negative stative statement

III. DIALOGS

1. Keala and Kanani

Keala: Greetings (between you and me).
Kanani: Yes, hi.
Keala: What's your name?

Kanani:	My name is Kanani. And you?
Keala:	My name is Keala.
Kanani:	How are you, Keala?
Keala:	I'm fine, thanks. And you?
Kanani:	I'm kind of sick.
Keala:	Too bad! Go to Doctor Kekuni!
Kanani:	Is he a good doctor?
Keala:	Yes, a very smart doctor.
Kanani:	Thanks. Bye.
Keala:	Bye. Take good care of your body.
Kanani:	You too.

2. The teacher and Kalae

The teacher:	Good afternoon, Kalae.
Kalae:	Hello, teacher.
The teacher:	How are you?
Kalae:	Fine. And you?
The teacher:	I'm rather tired.
Kalae:	Too bad! How are the students?
The teacher:	Tsā! They are really sulky.
Kalae:	Why?
The teacher:	The class is over, but the work isn't finished.
Kalae:	Are they lazy students?
The teacher:	Yes, they are very lazy.
Kalae:	Give them an "F."

3. Kanoe and Lehua

Kanoe:	Good morning, Lehua.
Lehua:	Hi, Kanoe. Come and eat breakfast.
Kanoe:	Thanks, but my stomach is full.
Lehua:	Drink some fruit juice.
Kanoe:	Yes, thanks. This is a really hot morning.
Lehua:	Yes, the sun is really hot. How's the family?
Kanoe:	We're fine, but the kids are kind of sulky.
Lehua:	Goodness! Why?
Kanoe:	The summer is over.
Lehua:	Too bad! Give this banana bread to them.
Kanoe:	You're a nice woman, Lehua. Thanks a lot.
Lehua:	You're welcome. Bye.
Kanoe:	Bye. You take care.
Lehua:	You too.

IV. ANSWERS

A. 1. au
    2. mākou
    3. mākou
    4. lākou
    5. lāua
    6. ʻo ia
    7. au
    8. māua
    9. mākou
    10. ʻoukou
    11. mākou
    12. kākou

B. Ke kumu: Pehea ʻoukou, e nā haumana?
    Nā haumana: ʻAno ʻōmaʻimaʻi mākou, e ke kumu.
    Ke kumu: Aloha ʻino! E noho iho ʻoukou.
    Nā haumana: Mahalo. He kumu ʻoluʻolu ʻoe.
    Ke kumu: ʻAe. E Kanani, e kiʻi aku ʻoe i ke kauka.
    Nā haumana: No ke aha mai?
    Ke kumu: He mau haumana ʻōmaʻimaʻi ʻoukou.
    Nā haumana: ʻAʻole, ʻaʻole. Maikaʻi nō mākou.
    Ke kumu: Tsā! Moloā loa ʻoukou. E hoʻi aku i ka hale. Pau
                  ka papa.
    Nā haumana: A hui hou. E mālama pono ʻoe.

C. 1. Liʻiliʻi kēlā moʻo.
    2. He moʻo liʻiliʻi kēlā.
    3. ʻOno loa kēia palaoa.
    4. He palaoa ʻono loa kēia.
    5. He kauka māluhiluhi ʻo ia.
    6. Māluhiluhi ke kauka.
    7. Wela kēia lā.
    8. He lā wela kēia.
    9. He ʻohana hauʻoli kēia.
    10. Hauʻoli kēia ʻohana.
    11. Nuha kēlā pōpoki.
    12. He pōpoki nuha ʻo Morris.
    13. He pōhaku nui loa kēnā.
    14. Nui loa kēnā pōhaku.
    15. Moloā ka ʻīlio.
    16. He ʻīlio moloā ʻo Poki.

D. 1. kāua
    2. kākou
    3. ʻoe
    4. au
    5. ʻolua
    6. māua
    7. ʻoukou
    8. mākou

6

HAʻAWINA ʻEONO

I. TOPICS

A. Simple verb sentences
B. *E* infinitive
C. *I/ma*
D. *Ke/ka* without English occurrence
E. Days of the week
F. *Mā*

II. BASIC SENTENCE TARGETS

1. Simple verb sentence with destination
2. Simple verb sentence with two locations
3. Time phrase; simple verb sentence with destination
4. Stative verb; *mā;* infinitive
5. Compound sentence; destination; time phrase; *ma hope iho;* simple verb sentence with direct object
6. Simple verb sentence; compound direct object; *ka* without English occurrence
7. Farewell with pronoun and time phrase

III. DIALOGS

1. At the university

Lokelani:	Good afternoon, Lilinoe.
Lilinoe:	Hi Lokelani. How are you?
Lokelani:	I'm really happy, thanks.

Lilinoe: Really? Why?
Lokelani: This is Friday, and school is over.
Lilinoe: Yes, that's good. Do you live in the dormitory?
Lokelani: Yes, but on Friday, I go back home to Nānākuli.
Lilinoe: You're so lucky! Does your family live in Nānākuli?
Lokelani: Yes, my father and mother live there.
Lilinoe: Too bad my family lives in Hilo.
Lokelani: What a pity! Visit my house! My family is happy to see my friends.
Lilinoe: Thanks, Loke. You're a really nice woman!

2. Lei and Kua'āina (country bumpkin)

Lei: Good morning.
Kua'āina: Good morning!
Lei: What's your name?
Kua'āina: My name is Kua'āina. And you?
Lei: Hi, Kua'āina. I'm Lei.
Kua'āina: I'm happy to meet you.
Lei: Me too. Do you live in Honolulu?
Kua'āina: No. I live in Kahalu'u, but my cousin lives in Honolulu.
Lei: What's her name?
Kua'āina: Lokelani Kamanu is her name.
Lei: For goodness sake! We live together in the dorm.
Kua'āina: Really! Do you go to the university?
Lei: Yes. Come visit us on Sunday.
Kua'āina: I go to church, but afterwards, okay.
Lei: Good. Goodbye until Sunday.
Kua'āina: Tell Loke hi. Take care.

IV. ANSWERS

A. Hi. My name is Lokelani Kamanu. I go to the University of Hawaii at Mānoa. I'm a new student. I live in the dorm. We eat at the cafeteria at Hale Kahawai. The food is kind of tasty, but not really delicious. My father and my mother live in Nānākuli. On Friday, I go back to the house in Nānākuli. Papa "guys" are really happy to see me. They prepare really delicious food, and we eat together. On Saturday, I help them to clean the house and the yard. In the evening we go out to the Chinese restaurant to eat dinner. Afterwards, we go back home to watch television. We go to church on Sunday, and afterwards, we eat brunch. Papa makes pancakes and Portuguese sausage. Papa drinks coffee, Mama drinks koko'olau tea, and I drink fruit juice. In the afternoon, I go back to the dorm to study. Too bad the weekend is over.

1. 'A'ole. He haumana 'o ia.
2. 'A'ole. Noho 'o ia ma ka hale noho haumana.
3. 'A'ole. Noho lāua ma Nānākuli.
4. 'Ano 'ono ka mea 'ai ma ke kula nui, akā, 'a'ole 'ono loa.
5. 'A'ole. Ho'i aku 'o ia i ka hale i ka Pō'alima.
6. 'A'ole. 'Ai lākou i ka hale 'aina Pākē.
7. 'A'ole. Hele lākou i ka hale pule.
8. 'A'ole. 'Ai lākou i ka 'aina awakea ma ka hale.
9. 'A'ole. Inu 'o ia i ke kī koko'olau.
10. 'A'ole. Ho'i 'o ia i ka 'auinalā i ka Lāpule.

For exercises C and D, where either *i* or *ma* is acceptable, both are written, separated by /. The first of each pair is the one I would use in my idiolect. Please note that / indicates an "either . . . or" situation; do not use both *i* and *ma* next to each other!

C. 1. Nānā mākou i/iā "Saturday Night Live" ma/i ke kīwī i/ma ka hale noho haumana.
   2. Noho ko'u hoahānau i/ma ka Hale Kuahine, a kipa au iā ia i/ma laila.
   3. 'Ike au i kou hoa aloha i/ma ka papa 'ōlelo Hawai'i.
   4. 'Ai pū 'o Mele mā i ka 'aina awakea i ka pā.
   5. Pi'i a'e 'o Nāhoa mā i nā pali ma/i Ko'olau Loa.

D. 1. Hana ko'u makuahine ma/i ka hale 'aina i/ma ke kula nui.
   2. Nānā a'e ka pōpoki i nā mo'o i/ma ka pōhaku.
   3. E 'olu'olu 'oe, e kipa mai ia'u ma/i ka hale noho haumana.
   4. Noho ko'u hoa aloha ma/i Kalihiwai i/ma ka mokupuni 'o Kaua'i.
   5. 'A'ole 'ono loa ka mea 'ai ma/i ke kula nui.

E. 1. Ho'oponopono 'o Pāpā mā i ka pā i ka Pō'aono.
   2. E aloha aku iā Lili mā.
   3. Pehea 'o Māmā mā?
   4. 'Ano 'ōma'ima'i 'o Nālani mā.
   5. E Keoki, e ki'i aku 'oe iā Pōmaika'i mā.

F. 1. Holoholo nā keiki i ka hopena pule.
    2. Hoʻomākaukau koʻu makua kāne i ka ʻaina awakea i ka Lāpule.
    3. Hoʻopaʻa haʻawina pū māua i ke ahiahi.
    4. Aloha a hui hou aku kākou i ka papa i ka Pōʻakahi.
    5. I ke kakahiaka, hele iho ka lawaiʻa i ke kai.

G. 1. E nā haumana, e hele i ka papa e hoʻoponopono i nā noho!
    2. Hele ʻo ia i ka hale pule e mālama i nā keiki liʻiliʻi.
    3. Hoʻi mai ʻo Pāpā i ka hale e ʻai i ka ʻaina awakea.
    4. Hauʻoli loa au e ʻike iā ʻoukou.
    5. Noho ʻo ia i ka hale e nānā iā Oprah Winfrey i ke kakahiaka.

H. 1. Inu ʻo Māmā mā i ke kī kokoʻolau.
    2. ʻAi mākou i ka iʻa i ka Pōʻalima.
    3. I ke ahiahi, ʻike mākou i ka moʻo nui i ka hale.
    4. Maikaʻi ka hana.
    5. I ka lā wela, ʻai mākou i ka ʻaina ahiahi i ka hale ʻaina.

REVIEW 1

HOʻI HOPE ʻEKAHI

I. ANSWERS

A. 1. kēnā   6. mākou
    2. kēia   7. ʻo
    3. kēlā   8. ʻolua
    4. ʻo ia   9. mā
    5. ʻoe   10. nā

B. 1. c; a has the wrong marker; b has no marker
    2. a; b and c have the wrong marker
    3. b; a has the wrong word order; c doesn't have *he*
    4. a; b and c have the wrong marker
    5. c; a has the wrong marker; b has no marker
    6. c; a ignores the impact of *nā;* b doesn't include the speaker in the pronoun
    7. a; b doesn't have a marker; c has the wrong marker
    8. c; a and b have the wrong marker
    9. b; a has no article; c has the wrong article
    10. a; b has no article; c has the wrong article
    11. a; b and c have the wrong marker
    12. b; a and c have the wrong marker

C. 1. ʻO wai kou makua kāne?
    2. ʻO Keliʻi koʻu makua kāne.
    3. He kumu kula ʻo ia.
    4. He kauka koʻu makuahine.
    5. ʻO ka Pōʻakahi kēia. ʻO kēia ka Pōʻakahi.
    6. He hale pule nui kēlā.

7. He pā ʻoluʻolu loa kēia.
8. ʻO koʻu hoahānau ʻo ia. ʻO ia koʻu hoahānau.
9. ʻO ka puke ʻōlelo Hawaiʻi kēnā.
10. ʻO kona hoa aloha ke kauka.

D. 1. Hana pū koʻu ʻohana e hoʻoponopono i ka hale i ka hopena pule.
2. Ma hope iho, holoholo mākou i Hanauma e luʻu iho.
3. Piʻi aʻe nā lawaiʻa i nā pali e nānā aʻe (or iho) i ke kai.
4. Nuha loa nā keiki kāne moloā.
5. E hāʻawi aku ʻoe i kēia palaoa i nā manu i ka pā.
6. Hauʻoli kona makua kāne a me kona makuahine e ʻike iā ia.
7. E ʻoluʻolu ʻoe, e hana i ke kope a me ke kī.
8. ʻOno ka pia i ka lā wela.
9. E kipa mai ʻoukou iaʻu ma koʻu hale i Māʻili.
10. Hana kēlā wahine Pukikī i ka palaoa ʻono.

E. 1. ʻO; ʻAlapaki is my father.
2. E; Students, come!
3. ʻo; mā; Loke folks live in Nānākuli.
4. ʻO; What's his name?
5. ʻo; i; i; Papa prepares pancakes on Sunday.
6. E; i; iā; Loke, give the kokoʻolau tea to Mama.
7. e; Here's the tea, Mama!
8. i; Say hi to the family.
9. iā; You-all help him.
10. i; They study in the evening.
11. ma; i; My friend eats at my house on the weekend.
12. i; i; I return to Hilo in the summer.
13. i; The birds drink nectar.

7

HAʻAWINA ʻEHIKU

I. TOPICS

A. *Ua*
B. *Mau* with determiners
C. *E* imperative with *kāua/kākou*
D. *Mai* (from)
E. Class inclusion and equational sentences with prepositional phrases
F. *Nui ka/nui nā:* there's a lot of _____

II. BASIC SENTENCE TARGETS

1. *Ua* with intransitive verb; *nehinei*
2. *Ua* with stative verb
3. Stative verb; *mau* with determiner
4. *E* imperative with *kāua*
5. *Mai* (from); *mai* (directional with noun)
6. Class-inclusion sentence with prepositional phrase
7. Equational sentence with prepositional phrase; *nei* with place name
8. *Nui nā/* there's a lot of _____
9. *Ia* as subject = it

III. DIALOGS

1. Nuku invites Kekailoa to surf

Nuku: Kekailoa, let's go surfing this afternoon.
Kekailoa: I went yesterday.
Nuku: Go again!

Kekailoa:	Cannot. Mama "folks" are really mad.
Nuku:	Why?
Kekailoa:	I went surfing, but the work at home wasn't done.
Nuku:	For goodness sake! You are really stupid.
Kekailoa:	Yes. My father said, "You stay quietly at home!"
Nuku:	If that's the case, lend me your new surfboard, please.
Kekailoa:	Okay, but take good care of the board. It's a really expensive one.
Nuku:	No problem. I'm a very skilled person.
Kekailoa:	Tsā! You're a clumsy person. Surf with your own board.

2. Leilehua telephones Mēlia

Leilehua:	Good morning. I want to speak to Mēlia.
Mēlia:	This is me. How are you, Leilehua?
Leilehua:	Goodness! You knew my voice. I'm fine today. And you?
Mēlia:	I'm really happy, because the kids went back to school this morning.
Leilehua:	And how about it? Are they happy?
Mēlia:	No. They're rather sulky.
Leilehua:	Why indeed?
Mēlia:	They want to play in the yard and swim in the sea.
Leilehua:	Tsā! Kids are very lazy these days. Summer is over, playing all day is over.
Mēlia:	Yes, you're so right. And I'm really happy to stay quietly at home.
Leilehua:	Me too. Wow, my father came back to eat, but lunch isn't ready. Bye.
Mēlia:	Yeah, bye.

3. Leilehua prepares lunch

Leilehua:	Papa, come and eat. Lunch is ready.
Papa:	Let's eat together!
Leilehua:	I ate this morning, and my stomach is full.
Papa:	No problem. Eat again. This fish is delicious.
Leilehua:	My friends brought enenue, salt, and limu kohu from Kauaʻi.
Papa:	And you made enenue poke with these things?
Leilehua:	Yes. I prepared the poke with these things and ʻinamona. This is a common dish (food) on Kauaʻi.
Papa:	Really? They're lucky. McDonald's is the common place to eat here in Honolulu.
Leilehua:	Too bad; you're right.

4. Leilehua invites Mēlia to lunch

Leilehua: Mēlia, let's eat dinner together at my house.
Mēlia: Okay, thanks. Today?
Leilehua: Yes. My cousins came from Hilo yesterday. They brought
            these goodies.
Mēlia: Japanese fishcake?
Leilehua: Yes, and ʻopihi from Keaukaha, jerked beef from
            Pāpaʻaloa, and breadfruit poi.
Mēlia: These foods from Hawaiʻi are really famous, but ʻopihi is
            kind of expensive, isn't it?
Leilehua: Yes, very expensive. But my cousins went to gather ʻopihi
            at Keaukaha and they were really lucky. There was a lot of
            ʻopihi.
Mēlia: We're lucky to eat these dishes. Bye until this evening.
Leilehua: Bye.

IV. ANSWERS

A. 1. Ua mākaukau ka ʻaina kakahiaka; mai e ʻai.
    2. Ua pipiʻi loa ka pipi kaula i kēia mau lā.
    3. Ua kaulana loa ka meaʻono iʻa Kepanī mai Hilo.
    4. Uaʻono loa kēia palaoa hou mai Molokaʻi mai.
    5. Ua mākaukau nā keiki e hele aku i ke kula.
    6. Ua mālie ke kai i ka Lāpule.
    7. Ua lāki nō kākou ma Hawaiʻi nei.
    8. Ua hemahema loa koʻu hoahānau ma ka papa heʻenalu.
    9. Ua maʻa ʻoe i ka mea ʻai Hawaiʻi?
    10. Ua moloā ka ʻohana apau i kēia kakahiaka.

B. 1. Ua hele koʻu ʻohana i Kauaʻi i kēia kau wela.
    2. Ua noho mākou i ka hale nui ma Kīlauea.
    3. Ua heʻenalu nā keiki i ka lā apau ma Kalihiwai.
    4. Ua pāʻani nā keiki liʻiliʻi i i ke one.
    5. Ua kuʻi ʻopihi ʻo Pāpā mā ma nā pōhaku nui.
    6. Ua hoʻomākaukau koʻu mau hoahānau i ka ʻaina awakea.
    7. Ua lawe mai lākou i ka poke, ka limu kohu, a me ka paʻakai.
    8. Ua ʻai nui mākou i ka mea ʻai Hawaiʻi.
    9. Ua makemake koʻu mau mākua e ʻai i ka palaoa kaulana mai
       Kīlauea.
    10. Ua holoholo aku lāua i Kīlauea e kiʻi i ka palaoa a me ka
        meaʻono.

C. 1. kona mau hoa aloha moloā
    2. kou mau hoahānau Kepanī
    3. ko'u mau ka'a kahiko
    4. kēia mau lā mālie
    5. kēlā mau mea 'ai ma'a mau
    6. kēlā mau papa he'enalu pipi'i
    7. ko'u mau mākua
    8. kēia mau mokupuni nani
    9. kona mau lole nani
   10. kēnā mau lei nani

D. 1. E Kekailoa, e 'ai kāua i ka hale 'aina Kepanī i kēia ahiahi.
    2. E hele kākou i ka he'enalu i ka Pō'aono.
    3. E Leilehua, e kipa aku kāua i kou mau hoa aloha ma Kaua'i.
    4. E nā keiki, e pā'ani kākou i ka pā.
    5. E Pāpā, e ho'omākaukau kāua i ka 'aina kakahiaka.

E. 1. Ua ho'i aku 'o Kalā mā i Kaua'i mai ko'u hale aku i nehinei.
    2. Ua hā'awi mai lākou i kēia pa'akai maika'i mai Hanapēpē mai.
    3. Ua kono ko'u mau mākua i ko'u mau hoahānau e hele mai mai
       Moloka'i mai.
    4. E lawe mai 'oe i kou papa he'enalu pono'ī mai kou hale mai.
    5. 'Ano hemahema nā kānaka mai Kansas i ka 'au'au kai.

F. 1. He mea 'ai ma'a mau ka poi 'ulu ma Hilo.
    2. 'O ka pipi kaula ka mea 'ai pipi'i loa ma kēia hale 'aina
       Hawai'i.
    3. He kanaka kaulana loa 'o Tom Selleck ma Hawai'i nei.
    4. He kumu 'ōlelo Hawai'i ko'u makuahine ma ke kula nui.
    5. 'O St. Andrew's Cathedral ka hale pule nui loa ma Honolulu.

In exercise G, where *ma/i* occurs, use one or the other. Do not use both
words at the same time.

G. 1. Nui nā haumana ma/i ke kula nui i Mānoa.
    2. Nui nā ka'a ma/i Ala Moana.
    3. Nui ka hana ma/i ke kula.
    4. Nui ke aloha ma/i ko'u hale pule.
    5. Nui nā kānaka ma/i McDonald's i ka lā apau.

8

HA‘AWINA ‘EWALU

I. TOPICS

A. *E* verb *ana* sentences
B. Sibling terms
C. Compound (dual and plural) subjects and objects
D. *Maiā*

II. BASIC SENTENCE TARGETS

1. Dual subject; *kaikaina* (female)
2. Dual subject; *kaikaina* (male)
3. Dual subject; *kaikua‘ana* (female)
4. Dual subject; *kaikua‘ana* (male)
5. Plural subject; *kaikunāne*
6. Plural subject; *kaikuahine*
7. *E* verb *ana* sentence; *i hea*
8. Class-inclusion sentence; *maiā* with name
9. *E* verb *ana* sentence; *maiā* with *ia*
10. *E* verb *ana* sentence; *aha* as verb
11. *E* verb *ana* sentence; *kēlā ‘apōpō*

III. DIALOGS

1. The Ikaika family

Lilinoe: Hi. I'm the oldest. I live in Hilo. Luika and Pualani are my younger sisters. ‘Alapaki, Kimo, and Lopaka are my brothers.

24

Luika: Hi. My name is Luika. I live in Honolulu. Lilinoe is my older sister. Pualani is my younger sister. 'Alapaki, Kimo, and Lopaka are my brothers.

Pualani: Hi. I'm the youngest. I live in Honolulu. Lilinoe and Luika are my older sisters. 'Alapaki, Kimo, and Lopaka are my brothers.

'Alapaki: Hi. I'm 'Alapaki. I live in Hilo. Kimo and Lopaka are my younger brothers. Lilinoe, Luika, and Pualani are my sisters.

Kimo: Hi. My name is Kimo. I live in Hilo. 'Alapaki is my older brother. Lopaka is my younger brother. Lilinoe, Luika, and Pualani are my sisters.

Lopaka: Hi. I'm Lopaka. I live in Hilo. 'Alapaki and Kimo are my older brothers. Lilinoe, Luika, and Pualani are my sisters.

2. On the street in Honolulu

Nanea: Hey, Pualani. Where are you going?
Pualani: I'm going to visit my grandma "folks." Let's go together.
Nanea: Okay, thanks. What's that big bundle?
Pualani: These are some presents from Lilinoe.
Nanea: Who is she?
Pualani: My older sister. She's living in Hilo.
Nanea: You're taking those things from her to your grandparents?
Pualani: Yes. They like koko'olau tea and saloon pilot crackers from Hilo.

3. On the telephone in Honolulu

Pualani: Luika, please pick up the kids at school this afternoon.
Luika: Okay. What's your problem?
Pualani: I'm going to the doctor.
Luika: Goodness! Are you pregnant again?
Pualani: No way! My hand is sore.
Luika: Soak your hand in hot water with salt.
Pualani: I did (it) like that, but the pain didn't stop.
Luika: For goodness sake! You take care!
Pualani: Yes, I'm going to the doctor.
Luika: Good. Afterwards, come to my house and eat dinner with the kids.
Pualani: Thanks a lot, Luika. You're a kindhearted big sister.

4. ʻAlapaki is staying at his home in Hilo

Haunani: ʻAlapaki, what are you doing?
ʻAlapaki: I'm looking at these pictures.
Haunani: Oh how beautiful! Who is this woman?
ʻAlapaki: My sister Pua.
Haunani: Does she live here in Hilo?
ʻAlapaki: No. She's living in Honolulu.
Haunani: What is she doing there?
ʻAlapaki: She's a Hawaiian language teacher at the university in Mānoa.
Haunani: Is she the youngest?
ʻAlapaki: Yes, and Lilinoe is the oldest. Let's go have lunch at her restaurant.
Haunani: Okay! Let's go!

5. On the street in Hilo

Nīele: Lopaka, what are you doing?
Lopaka: I'm waiting for ʻAlapaki "guys."
Nīele: Are they your older brothers?
Lopaka: Yes. We're going to visit Lilinoe, my sister. Let's go together.
Nīele: Thanks, but (it's) not possible. Mama is preparing lunch and I'm going back to eat.
Lopaka: Give my regards to Mama "folks." Bye.
Nīele: Yes, take care.

6. In Hilo

Noelani: Lilinoe, has your grandmother arrived from Honolulu?
Lilinoe: No. She is coming tomorrow.
Noelani: How about your grandfather? Is he coming?
Lilinoe: No. He is staying with Luika "folks." There's a lot of rain in Hilo, and his bones hurt.
Noelani: Too bad! That's a pity. I really like heavy rain.
Lilinoe: Me too. Sleeping is really good on a rainy night.

IV. ANSWERS

B.   Ma ke kelepona:

Kaulu: E holoholo ana mākou i ka Pōʻaono. E hele pū kākou!
Pua: ʻAʻole hiki. E hoʻoponopono ana au i ka hale. E hiki mai ana
         koʻu kaikuaʻana mai Hilo mai i ka Lāpule i ka ʻauinalā.
Kaulu: E hoʻoponopono i ka hale i ke kakahiaka.
Pua: E hele ana au i ka hale pule i ka awakea, a e ʻai ana mākou i
         ka ʻaina awakea i laila. Ma hope iho, e kiʻi ana au iā ia.
Kaulu: E hoʻoponopono pū kāua i ka hale i ka Pōʻaono, a ma hope e
         holoholo kāua!
Pua: Mahalo a nui loa, e Kaulu. He hoa aloha maikaʻi ʻoe.

C.   1. ʻO Lilinoe ka hiapo.
     2. ʻO Pua ka muli loa.
     3. ʻAʻole. E noho ana ʻo ia i Honolulu.
     4. ʻAe. E noho ana ʻo Lilinoe i Hilo.
     5. ʻAʻole. E noho ana ʻo Pua i Honolulu.
     6. ʻAe. E noho ana kona mau kaikunāne i Hilo.
     7. ʻAʻole. Hana ʻo ia i kona hale ʻaina.
     8. ʻAʻole hāpai hou ʻo Pualani.
     9. ʻAe. Kōkua ʻo Luika e kiʻi i nā keiki a mālama iā lākou.
    10. ʻAʻole. E noho ana ʻo Tūtū Kāne me Luika mā.

D.

Nanea: Hūi, e Pua, e hele ana ʻoe i hea?
Pua: E lawe aku ana au i kēia pūʻolo i koʻu mau kūpuna. He
         makana ia mai koʻu mau kaikunāne.
Nanea: He mea ʻai mai Hilo mai?
Pua: ʻAe, ʻo ka pelena poepoe. E kali ana ʻo Tūtū mā i kēia pelena
         maiā lākou mai. Kū lāua i ka pelena i ke kope.
Nanea: He hana maʻa mau kēlā. A ʻono loa!
Pua: E hele mai e ʻai i ka ʻaina kakahiaka i kēlā ʻapōpō. Nui nā
         pelena ma koʻu hale.
Nanea: Mahalo a nui loa. A hui hou i kēlā apōpō.

9
HAʻAWINA ʻEIWA

I. TOPICS

A. K-possessives; *O/A*-categories
B. *Aia* locational sentences
C. *Hea; i hea*
D. Word order in verb clauses
E. Hawaiian verbless sentences with possessives
F. *Māua ʻo* _____

II. BASIC SENTENCE TARGETS

1. *Aia* locational sentence with *he; ko* Name
2. *Aia* locational sentence with *ka*
3. *Aia* locational sentence; *hea* modifier
4. *Aia* locational sentence with time phrase
5. *Aia* locational question
6. *Aia* locational sentence; *ko* possessive with noun phrase
7. *Eia* locational sentence
8. Verb clause word order; possessive with plural *mau*
9. Verb clause word order
10. Verbless sentence
11. Verbless sentence
12. *Māua ʻo X*

III. DIALOGS

1. At Keola "folks" house in Honolulu

Keola: Mēlia, read this letter from Hilo.
Mēlia: The Ikaika family has invited us to go to Hilo!
Keola: Yes. There's a party at Lilinoe's restaurant.
Mēlia: Yes, yes, I read it. It's Mama Ikaika's birthday.
Keola: Her grandson is coming from San Francisco.
Mēlia: All the grandchildren are coming to see their grandmother.
Keola: This is a happy occasion. What day is the party?
Mēlia: The party is next week on Friday and Saturday.
Keola: On two days?
Mēlia: There's a family party at the Chinese restaurant on Friday, and there's a lūʻau on Saturday. They invited us to go to the two evenings.
Keola: We're so lucky! I'll call the airlines.

2. At the Chinese restaurant in Hilo

Mēlia: Lilinoe, Keola and I are very happy to meet your mother. Her bones are so strong. (She is so healthy.)
Lilinoe: Yes, we are really blessed. Our parents are still living, and their bodies are really strong.
Mēlia: And how about the grandparents? Are they all still living?
Lilinoe: Yes, our grandfolks on (our) mother's side are in Honolulu. They are living with my younger sister, Luika.
Mēlia: And how about Papa's parents? Are they living here in Hilo?
Lilinoe: Yes, they are living here in Hilo with their daughter, my aunty. She's the oldest.
Mēlia: Did the whole family come to Hilo this weekend?
Lilinoe: Yes, we are all here at this restaurant this evening.
Mēlia: Truly? This is a very happy evening.

3. At Lilinoe's restaurant in Hilo

ʻAlapaki: Mēlia, go and get some food. Everything is on the table.
Mēlia: Thanks, ʻAlapaki. I'm waiting for my husband. He's parking the car, and he's coming right back again.
ʻAlapaki: Did you rent a car?
Mēlia: Our son loaned his car; he's in Honokaʻa now. Oh, here's my husband. We'll eat now.
ʻAlapaki: Good. Eat up; there's a lot of food.

Mēlia:	Keola, I'm going to prepare your plate. What do you want?
Keola:	Mahalo, Mēlia. I want kālua pig, chicken, squid lū'au, lomi salmon, and all the raw stuff.
Mēlia:	Okay. The poi, the sweet potato, the pineapple and the drinks are on the table.
Keola:	Yes, and the haupia, kūlolo, and the cake are on that table over there.
Mēlia:	This is a very good lū'au.

4. At Pua's Hawaiian language class at the university at Mānoa

Kulia:	No'eau, where are all the students?
No'eau:	They're at the teacher's house.
Kulia:	Did Pua come back from Hilo?
No'eau:	Yes, and she invited us to eat lunch at her house.
Kulia:	What are we eating?
No'eau:	All Hawaiian food. She's preparing kālua pig and cabbage.
Kulia:	What? Did she bring the leftovers from their party in Hilo? I crave the raw stuff.
No'eau:	Me too! Let's go quickly!

IV. ANSWERS

A.
1. ko Tūtū lā hānau
2. ka'u pōpoki
3. ko mākou mau kaikunāne
4. kā ka 'īlio mau iwi
5. kāna leka
6. kā lāua kaikamahine
7. kā 'olua pū'olo
8. ko Lilinoe ka'a
9. kā 'Alapaki keiki kāne
10. kā Garfield 'aina ahiahi
11. kā kākou pā'ina
12. kā lākou mau pā
13. kā Tūtū kāne mau mo'opuna
14. ko ka pua'a ola
15. kou aloha
16. ko ka moa hale
17. kā ka hui lū'au
18. kona ikaika
19. ko māua hau'oli
20. kā ke kauka waiwai

B.
1. E Mēlia, eia he kono maiā Lilinoe mā.
2. Aia kā Tūtū wahine lū'au i kēia pule a'e.
3. Aia ka pā'ina ma ko 'Alapaki hale.
4. Eia kā ka mo'opuna makana.
5. Aia ko'u ka'a ma ke ala nui.
6. Aia i hea ka hala kahiki a me ka mea'ono?

7. Aia nā meaʻono apau mā kēlā pākaukau maʻō.
8. Aia kou lā hānau i ka lā hea?
9. Aia kā kākou papa i ka hale hea?
10. Eia au me ka puaʻa kālua me ke kāpiki. E ʻai kākou!

C. 1. E kono ana māua ʻo kaʻu kāne i kā ʻoukou papa i ka pāʻina.
2. E kali ana māua ʻo Lopaka iā Kimo.
3. Aia ʻo Kimo lāua ʻo ʻAlapaki ma ko Lilinoe hale ʻaina.
4. Ua hiki mai māua ʻo kēlā haumana mai Hilo mai ma kēlā mokulele maʻō.
5. E hele aku ana māua ʻo kaʻu moʻopuna i Kapalakiko i kēia makahiki aʻe.
6. E kiʻi ana ʻo Kimo a me kāna mau keiki kāne i ka heʻe.

D. 1. E hoʻi hou mai ana nō lākou i kēlā ʻapōpō.
2. E ola mau ana nō ko mākou mau kūpuna apau.
3. E lawe mai ana nō ʻo ia i ke koena i ka papa.
4. E ʻai mau iho ana nō ka puaʻa i kā Tūtū mau ʻuala.
5. E hana nui ana nō ka ʻohana i ka lūʻau.

E. 1. He aha kāu mea inu?
2. He aha ko lākou pilikia?
3. He aha ko nā moʻopuna makemake?
4. He aha kāu hana?
5. He aha kā mākou haʻawina?

F. Haʻawina ʻElima

Exercise A. kā ʻoukou, koʻu, kaʻu, kaʻu, kaʻu, ko ʻoukou.

REVIEW 2
HOʻI HOPE ʻELUA

I. ANSWERS

A. 1. c   9. a
    2. c   10. c
    3. a   11. c
    4. c   12. c
    5. a   13. a
    6. b   14. b
    7. a   15. a
    8. b

B. 1. ko   7. ko
    2. kā   8. ko
    3. kā   9. ko
    4. ko   10. kā
    5. ko   11. kā
    6. ko   12. ko

C. 1. Kekai, let's go surfing.
    2. Let's all eat again!
    3. Mama "guys" are really mad.
    4. You recognized my voice.
    5. They want to play in the yard.
    6. Our work is done.
    7. Japanese fishcakes are common food in Hilo.
    8. There was a lot of trouble in class yesterday.
    9. What are your sisters doing?
    10. Kimo is carrying the packages from Lopaka to his car.
    11. Luika and I are waiting for our older sister.
    12. All our family will visit Tūtū kāne "folks" house.

13. There are lots of leftovers from our party.
14. My wife is parking the car over there.
15. Here comes our plane; let's go.
16. The sick pig is still living.
17. There's a really big exam this Thursday, but no problem. I'm really prepared.
18. Where's the club's lūʻau?
19. Their lūʻau is at the club's house in Waimānalo.
20. What building is our class in?

D. 1. He aha kā kākou hana?
   2. He aha kona makemake?
   3. He aha kā Mēlia mea ʻai?
   4. He aha ko lākou pilikia?
   5. He aha kāu mea inu?

E. 1. E hana ana ʻo Tūtū pā i ka heʻe maka me ka paʻakai a me ka inamona.
   2. Eia aʻe ka mokulele mai Kapalakiko mai.
   3. Hūi, e hele ʻāwīwī mai. Aia nā moa kāne i ka pā.
   4. ʻAʻole pilikia. Ua lawe aku ʻo Tūtū wahine iā lākou i laila i nehinei.
   5. E kiʻi ana ʻo ia iā lākou i ka lā ʻapōpō.
   6. Ua ʻai ʻoe i ka haupia me ka hala kahiki?
   7. E lawe mai ana koʻu mau hoahānau i ke kāmano mai Seattle mai i kēia pule aʻe.
   8. E hui mau ana nō ka Hui Kamaʻilio ma Mānoa Gardens i ka Pōʻahā.
   9. Makemake māua ʻo Lono e kipa i kou mau mākua.
   10. Ua ʻike māua iā lāua i ka hale ʻaina.
   11. Ikaika nō ko lāua mau iwi.
   12. E ola mau ana nō ko mākou mau kūpuna apau.
   13. Ua kū ʻo Kimo lāua ʻo Lopaka i ke kāmano i ka wai.
   14. E hiamoe ana ka muli loa i kona noho.
   15. Aloha ʻino; e hāpai ʻoe iā ia i koʻu kaʻa.
   16. ʻAʻole pilikia; eia aʻe kona kaikuaʻana.
   17. Ua ʻae mai ʻo Lilinoe i kona muʻumuʻu hou.
   18. ʻOiaʻiʻo nō? ʻO ia ka hiapo i kou ʻohana?
   19. ʻAe; he wahine lokomaikaʻi ʻo ia, a pōmaikaʻi nō hoʻi mākou.
   20. Kōkua ʻo ia i kona mau kaikaina i ka manawa apau.

10

HAʻAWINA ʻUMI

I. TOPICS

A. Negatives
B. Numbers
C. *E* imperative with *au, māua, mākou*
D. *Kēlā me kēia*
E. *Kuʻu*
F. *Aʻu*

II. BASIC SENTENCE TARGETS

1. Negative stative sentence
2. Negative stative with pronoun subject (optional *i*)
3. Negative past tense with common noun subject
4. Negative past tense with proper noun subject
5. Negative past tense with pronoun subject
6. Negative progressive with common noun subject
7. Negative progressive with proper noun subject
8. Negative progressive with pronoun subject
9. *E* imperative with *au*
10. *Kēlā me kēia*

III. DIALOGS

1. At the store at Ala Moana Center

Luika: I want to buy some black shoes, please.
Clerk: And what is the size of your shoe?
Luika: Size 10.

Clerk: Wow! Your feet are very long!
Luika: Yes, because I'm a very tall woman.
Clerk: I'll get the shoes.
Clerk: Here's some white shoes and red shoes.
Luika: I didn't want those colors.
Clerk: Excuse me. I didn't listen properly. I'll go again.
Luika: Tsā! He's a stupid person. I'm not waiting.

2. At Ala Moana Center

Pōmaika'i: Hey, Luika! You have a lot of packages.
Luika: Yes. I bought three new pairs of shoes and four mu'umu'u too.
Pōmaika'i: Really? Do you buy new clothes often?
Luika: No. And these things aren't really expensive. I went to all the really cheap stores.
Pōmaika'i: So how about it? Maybe two hundred dollars for these things?
Luika: Two hundred fifty dollars. But I won't buy clothes again this year.
Pōmaika'i: I'll carry your packages to your car.
Luika: Thanks, Pōmaika'i, but I didn't come by car.
Pōmaika'i: No problem. I'll take you in my car.
Luika: Thanks a lot; let's go eat lunch.
Pōmaika'i: Okay. What shall we eat?
Luika: There's delicious Korean food at Kim Chee II.
Pōmaika'i: Yeah, their beef and their chicken is really delicious. Let's go!

3. At the airport

Mealani: Hey Luika! Where are you going?
Luika: I'm going to Hilo to visit my grandma.
Mealani: Isn't your family living in Hilo now?
Luika: No. My husband and I moved to Honolulu in 1982.
Mealani: Wow! I haven't been back to the island of Hawai'i for twenty years.
Luika: Really! There are a lot of new stores there now. There are shopping centers everywhere.
Mealani: When I was a kid, not at all. But we didn't often go to buy stuff. There wasn't a lot of money.
Luika: Yeah, it was like that with us too. Here's my plane. Bye.
Mealani: Yes, give my aloha to Tūtū "folks."

4. On the phone

Lilinoe: Hi, Pua. Luika isn't going back to Honolulu tomorrow.
Pua: Really? Isn't she going to work?
Lilinoe: Yes, but it's no problem. There isn't a lot of business at her
            store at the moment.
Pua: Is she helping you in your restaurant?
Lilinoe: She's not working with me. She's helping Mama "guys."
Pua: What's their problem? Are they sick?
Lilinoe: They aren't sick; they're just kind of tired.
Pua: Too bad! Mama didn't tell me. I'll call her and give her my
            aloha.
Lilinoe: Yeah, that's a good idea.

5. At the university

Wahanui: Teacher, your students aren't writing the exam.
Pua: Really? Why? Aren't they ready?
Wahanui: Yeah, right. These lazy people didn't study. They haven't
            learned the numbers from one to one hundred.
Pua: Shame! They're not going to graduate from the university
            next year.
Wahanui: Oh my goodness! Their parents will be mad at them.
Pua: That's their problem! I'm not helping lazy students. They
            didn't come to class every day, and they missed out.
Wahanui: Yeah. And they didn't listen to the tapes. That's their
            major problem.
Pua: I think they'll all come to class next week.

IV. ANSWERS

A.   1. ʻAʻole ʻo ia e lawe mai ana i ka hala kahiki mai Molokaʻi mai.
         He's not bringing the pineapples from Molokaʻi.
      2. ʻAʻole i inu ka ʻohana i ka wai huaʻai. The family didn't drink
         fruit juice.
      3. ʻAʻole e hoʻolohe ana nā kamaliʻi i ka manu. The children
         aren't listening to the bird.
      4. ʻAʻole e haʻi mai ana kā mākou kumu i kona manaʻo. Our
         teacher isn't telling her opinion.
      5. ʻAʻole i kūʻai mai ʻo Kalei i ke kāmaʻa hou. Kalei didn't buy
         new shoes.

6. 'A'ole emi loa kēia mau lipine. These tapes aren't cheap.
7. 'A'ole lō'ihi loa kāu keiki kāne. Your son isn't very tall.
8. 'A'ole lākou mākaukau e kākau i ka hō'ike. They aren't prepared to write the exam.
9. 'A'ole au i hele pinepine i ka hale kū'ai i ku'u wā kamali'i. I didn't go to the store often when I was a kid.
10. 'A'ole kū'ai pinepine mai ko'u mau kūpuna i kēlā me kēia mea 'ai Hawai'i. My grandparents don't often buy all kinds of Hawaiian food.

B. 4. 'umikūmāhiku kanahikukūmāwalu
5. 'umikūmāwalu iwakālua

1. kanalimakūmāono
2. kanahikukūmālua
3. kanahākūmāiwa
4. kanakolukūmāhiku
5. 'umikūmāiwa
6. iwakāluakūmāwalu
7. 'umikūmākolu
8. ho'okahi haneli a me 'elima
9. 'elua haneli kanakolukūmākolu
10. ho'okahi kaukani, 'ehā haneli, kanaonokūmālua
11. kanaiwakūmāono
12. kanawalukūmāhā
13. 'elima haneli, kanahākūmākahi
14. 'eiwa kaukani, 'eiwa haneli
15. 'ekolu haneli a me 'eono

1. 16
2. 48
3. 31
4. 708
5. 150
6. 687
7. 505
8. 2,495
9. 39
10. 26

C. 1. E ha'i aku au iā lākou e hele.
2. E 'olu'olu, e kū'ai i kēia mau na'aukake Pukikī.
3. Hiki nō, e kū'ai mai nō māua.
4. E ho'olohe pono nō mākou, e ke kumu.
5. E lawe aku au i nā kamali'i me a'u.

D. 1. I ko mākou wā kamaliʻi, ua ʻai mākou i kēlā me kēia mea ʻai.
    2. Holoholo nā kūpuna i ke kikowaena Ala Moana i kēlā me kēia
       lā.
    3. Ua hoʻolohe māua ʻo Kawehi i kēlā me kēia lipine Hawaiʻi ma
       ka hale kūʻai, akā ʻaʻole mākou i kūʻai.
    4. ʻAʻole e kali ana ke kumu no kēlā me kēia haumana.
    5. Hele ʻo Māmā i ka hale kūʻai e nānā wale nō i kēlā me kēia
       mea.

E. 1. I kuʻu wā kamaliʻi, ʻaʻole au i mālama pono i kuʻu kino.
    2. Aloha nō au i kuʻu kupuna kāne.
    3. ʻAʻole i hiki mai kuʻu mau mākua me aʻu.
    4. ʻAʻole lōʻihi loa nā wāhine Kōlea.
    5. Ua neʻe mai ʻo Ferdinand lāua ʻo Imelda in Honolulu nei i ka
       makahiki ʻumikūmāiwa kanawalukūmāono.
    6. ʻAʻole hoka nā kānaka lokomaikaʻi.
    7. ʻAʻole ʻo ia i kūʻai i ke kāmaʻa ʻulaʻula.
    8. Ua kākau ʻo Lilinoe i ka leka i ka hale kūʻai kāmaʻa.
    9. Nui nā muʻumuʻu emi loa i ka Muʻumuʻu Factory.
   10. E puka aʻe ana kaʻu keiki kāne mai ka papa ʻeono i kēia maka-
       hiki aʻe.

11

HAʻAWINA ʻUMIKŪMĀKAHI

I. TOPICS

A. "Have-a" sentences
B. *Paha, nō hoʻi, wale nō*
C. Negative locational sentences: *ʻaʻohe* X

II. BASIC SENTENCE TARGETS

1. Have-a sentence with possessive pronouns
2. Have-a sentence with possessive pronouns
3. Have-a sentence with possessive noun
4. Have-a sentence with possessive proper noun
5. Have-a sentence with compound possessive
6. Have-a sentence with *mau*
7. Have-a sentence with *ko laila*
8. *Paha*
9. *Wahi*
10. Negative locational sentence

III. DIALOGS

1. On the phone in Honolulu

Luika: Pua, have you heard? Kimo "folks" have moved to Kona.
Pua: Really? I didn't hear. Why?
Luika: He has a job there.
Pua: What's his new job?
Luika: He's the manager of the macadamia nut plant in Nāpoʻopoʻo.

39

Pua: Do they have a house in Kona?
Luika: Yes, the macadamia company has a house. Kimo and Laua'e
          are living there.
Pua: Kona is a really hot place, isn't it?
Luika: Yes, but their house is cool. The wind blows all day.
Pua: And what? Does Laua'e have a job too?
Luika: Yes, she's working at the police station.
Pua: They're so lucky. I'll call them.
Luika: Here's their new phone number: 737-5824.
Pua: Thanks, Luika. Bye.

2. Pua calls Kimo

Pua: Hey Kimo, I heard you two have a new job in Kona.
Kimo: Yeah, right. And we have a new house too. Come visit this
          weekend.
Pua: Okay. We'll rent a car at the airport.
Kimo: No. I have a truck and Laua'e has a car. I'll pick you up. Do
          you have a cat?
Pua: We have a lot of cats. Do you want a cat?
Kimo: Bring two or three maybe. We have some big rats in the yard
          and the house too. They eat the macadamia nuts.
Pua: Tsa! Honolulu cats don't eat rats. They only eat cat food.
Kimo: Maybe so. I'll get a cat from Kailua.

3. At the university

Ha'aheo: 'Auli'i, you didn't come to school yesterday.
'Auli'i: Yes, I was kind of sick. I have a cold.
Ha'aheo: Too bad. Do you have a doctor in Honolulu?
'Auli'i: No. Maui is my birthplace. My doctor is there.
Ha'aheo: I have a really good doctor. Do you want his name?
'Auli'i: Yes, thanks. Do you have a pencil?
Ha'aheo: Yeah. I'll write his phone number on this paper.
'Auli'i: Where is this doctor?
Ha'aheo: He has an office in Kaimukī. Do you have a car?
'Auli'i: No. I'm going on the bus.
Ha'aheo: No way. I'll take you in my car. Maybe we should go this
          afternoon.
'Auli'i: You are a really good-hearted friend; I'll call the doctor.

4. In Tuti's class

'Eleu: Teacher, I have a question.
Tuti: Good, 'Eleu. I have some answers. What are your questions?
'Eleu: Do you have family on Niʻihau?
Tuti: Yes, my mother "folks" are there.
'Eleu: Do they have a phone?
Tuti: No way. Niʻihau is a tiny island.
'Eleu: Do they have a car?
Tuti: No. The bosses only have some trucks.
'Eleu: Maybe your family has a horse?
Tuti: No. They walk everywhere.
'Eleu: And what? There's a store on Niʻihau, isn't there?
Tuti: No. The people buy everything on Kauaʻi.
'Eleu: Oh my goodness! Does Niʻihau have a school?
Tuti: Yes. There's only a school, a church, and homes on Niʻihau.
'Eleu: And what? Does that place have a restaurant?
Tuti: No way. There aren't a lot of people on Niʻihau. They might number a hundred and fifty maybe. They always eat at home.
'Eleu: They have TV at home, don't they?
Tuti: 'Eleu, there's no electricity on Niʻihau; so there's no TV, no movies, no refrigerator, no hot water, no electric lights.
'Eleu: Wow! I thought I wanted to live on Niʻihau, but I might die. I'm not used to that life-style.
Tuti: That might be so. Living on Niʻihau is hard work.

IV. ANSWERS

A. 1. ko   6. kāu
    2. kāna   7. ko; kona
    3. kāna   8. kā lākou
    4. ko ʻolua   9. kā kākou
    5. kona   10. ko

B. 1. b
    2. a
    3. c
    4. b
    5. b

C. 1. He ʻiole make kēia.
    2. Make kēia ʻiole.
    3. He ʻiole make kā ka pōpoki.

4. He pahu hau nui kēlā.
5. Nui kēlā pahu hau.
6. He pahu hau nui kā ko'u 'ohana.
7. He wahine lokomaika'i ko'u kaikuahine.
8. He kaikuahine lokomaika'i ko'u.
9. He luna maika'i 'o ia.
10. Maika'i kāna luna.
11. He luna maika'i kāna.
12. He lio 'āwīwī 'o ia.
13. 'Āwīwī kona lio.
14. He lio 'āwīwī kona.

D. 1. 'A'ohe 'iole i ka hale me ka pōpoki.
2. 'A'ohe makani i kēia lā.
3. 'A'ohe kula i kēia pule a'e.
4. 'A'ohe papa 'ōlelo Hawai'i i nehinei.
5. 'A'ohe pane ma kēia pepa.
6. 'A'ohe ki'i'oni'oni i ke kakahiaka.
7. 'A'ohe hale ki'i'oni'oni ma ke mokupuni 'o Ni'ihau.
8. 'A'ohe hale ki'i'oni'oni nō ho'i ma Lāna'i.
9. 'A'ohe hale ki'i'oni'oni paha ma Moloka'i.
10. 'A'ohe ka'a lawe 'ohua ma Maui.

E. 1. Ua ne'e aku mākou mai ko makou 'āina hānau i ka makahiki 1980.
2. He kelepona ko ke ke'ena?
3. Aia paha ka luna ma/i ke ke'ena.
4. He uila ko Ni'ihau?
5. He hale hou ko ko'u kaikunāne i Kona.
6. He lā anu kēia, no ka mea, e pā mai ana ka makani.
7. He hana nui ka nohona ma Ni'ihau.
8. Hele wāwae nā kamali'i i kēlā me kēia wahi ma Ni'ihau.
9. Pipi'i loa ka uila ma ka mokupuni 'o Moloka'i.

12

HAʻAWINA ʻUMIKŪMĀLUA

I. TOPICS

A. K-less possessives
B. "Have-a-number" sentences
C. "Have-a-lot" sentences
D. *ʻEhia* as modifier
E. Telling one's age
F. *Hū ka* X!

II. BASIC SENTENCE TARGETS

1. Asking a person's age
2. Telling someone's age
3. "Have-how-many" question with possessive pronoun
4. "Have-a-number" sentence with possessive pronoun
5. "Have-how-many" question with possessive noun phrase
6. "Have-a-number" sentence with possessive proper name
7. "Have-only-one" sentence
8. "Have-a-lot" sentence with possessive pronoun
9. "Have-a-lot" sentence with possessive noun phrase
10. K-less possessive phrase
11. "Have-none" question
12. *ʻEhia* as modifer
13. *Hū ka* X!

III. DIALOGS

1. At Mama Ikaika's lūʻau

Keola: Aloha, Mrs. Ikaika. This is your "how many" birthday?
Mama: This is my sixty-fifth birthday. Yes, I'm sixty-five.
Keola: How wonderful! Your health is so good. How many children do you have?
Mama: We have six children, three boys, three girls.
Keola: And how many grandchildren do you have?
Mama: Goodness! We have a lot of grandchildren. We have maybe fourteen grandchildren.
Keola: How many children does Lilinoe, the oldest, have?
Mama: She doesn't have any children.
Keola: And what about the other daughters?
Mama: Luika has five kids, and Pua has two.
Keola: And how many children do the boys have?
Mama: ʻAlapaki has two, Kimo has four, and Lopaka has only one.

2. In Hilo

Nīele: Hey, Lilinoe. What are you doing?
Lilinoe: I'm going to my brother ʻAlapaki's house.
Nīele: What does he do?
Lilinoe: He's a farmer on homestead land in Panaʻewa. Their house is in Keaukaha.
Nīele: Really? I have family in Keaukaha. What's his wife's name?
Lilinoe: Her name is ʻEkekela. Her family name is Ahuna.
Nīele: That's it! Her mother is my cousin. Give her my regards.
Lilinoe: Yeah, okay. Bye.

3. At ʻAlapaki "folks" house

Kaleo: Hi, Aunty. Come inside.
Lilinoe: Thanks, Kaleolani. Goodness! You're so tall! How old are you?
Kaleo: I'm fifteen.
Lilinoe: Ho, I'm an old lady. How old is your sister?
Kaleo: Kuʻuipo is only five. Where is Uncle ʻApenela?
Lilinoe: He's at home. He's planting all kinds of stuff in the vegetable garden.
Kaleo: You don't have a flower garden?

Lilinoe: Yes, we have a flower garden, but it's full with all kinds of flowers.
Kaleo: Here's my friends. We're going to our teacher's house.
Lilinoe: Bye, Kaleo. You all be careful.
Kaleo: Yes. We won't drive fast.

4. At ʻAlapaki "folks" house

ʻEkekela: Lilinoe, excuse me. I didn't know you had come.
Lilinoe: No problem. Where's ʻAlapaki?
ʻEkekela: He went to Panaʻewa to plant sweet potato. You don't have work today?
Lilinoe: Yes, I'm working. I came to buy ʻopihi at ʻAwili store.
ʻEkekela: Shucks, they don't have ʻopihi. I called this morning.
Lilinoe: Tsā! That's a big problem. The ʻopihi is really expensive at the supermarket. One hundred thirty dollars for one gallon.
ʻEkekela: Wow, how expensive! Maybe there's ʻopihi in Nāpoʻopoʻo. Call Kimo!
Lilinoe: Yeah, that's a good idea. I'll call him.

IV. ANSWERS

B.   1. (He) kanalima ona makahiki.
     2. ʻO Go Go kona inoa.
     3. ʻO Wok Wok ka hiapo.
     4. ʻO Pau Pau ka muli loa.
     5. ʻEhā ona kaikuaʻana.
     6. ʻAʻohe ona kaikuaʻana.
     7. ʻAe, ʻekolu ona kaikaina.
     8. ʻEhā a lākou kaikuahine.
     9. ʻAe, ʻehā a lākou kaikunāne.
    10. ʻO Shoot Shoot kona inoa.
(Sentences 1, 5, 7, 8, and 9 can have *mau* before the noun.)

C.   1. ka helu kelepona a Lei mā
     2. nā nīnau a kēlā mau haumana moloā
     3. ka mala ʻai o kēlā mahiʻai
     4. ka wahine a koʻu ʻanakala
     5. ke ola kino o ka luahine
     6. ke kalaka o ka mākaʻi
     7. ke keʻena o kā mākou luna

8. ka inoa o kēlā mokupuni
9. ka ikaika o ka makani
10. ka ʻāina hoʻopulapula o ka ʻohana

D. 1. Ua neʻe lākou i ka hale o ko lākou mau mākua.
    2. E kanu ana ʻo ʻAnakala ʻApenela i ka ʻuala ʻē aʻe.
    3. Hū! Ka ʻono o kēia mea ʻai Kōlea!
    4. Hū! Ka nui o kou wāwae!
    5. Nui nā hala kahiki a ka luna haole i kona kalaka.

E. Hi. This is Lokelani Kamanu. Do you remember me? My family
    lives in Nānākuli, my birthplace. I don't have any older sisters, I
    don't have any younger sisters, I don't have any brothers. I am the
    only child in my family. But there are lots of chickens, pigs, dogs,
    and cats at our house. We don't have a horse, because horses are
    very expensive.
       I'm going back to Nānākuli this weekend because it is my grand-
    pa's birthday on Saturday. He is my mother's father. His body is
    still strong, and his health is also very good. He always works in the
    vegetable garden and the flower garden on the homestead land. He
    really likes to plant all kinds of things everywhere. He has a lot of
    very beautiful flowers. My grandma gets really mad because the
    yard is so full, and water is very expensive. Nānākuli is a very hot
    land. Grandpa waters the crops in the morning and evening every
    day. Wow, so much water, and wow, how mad Grandma gets!

F. 1. ʻAʻohe ona kaikuaʻana.
    2. ʻAʻohe ona kaikaina.
    3. ʻAʻohe ona kaikunāne.
    4. Hoʻokahi wale nō a lāua keiki. Hoʻokahi keiki wale nō a ko
       Lokelani mau mākua.
    5. Hana mau ʻo ia i ka māla ʻai a me ka māla pua.

REVIEW 3

HO‘I HOPE ‘EKOLU

I. ANSWERS

A. 1. ‘A‘ohe pua nani o ka māla pua.
       The flower garden doesn't have beautiful flowers.
    2. ‘A‘ole emi loa ka ‘uala i kēia manawa.
       Sweet potatoes are not very cheap nowadays.
    3. ‘A‘ole ‘o ia e kākau ana i kona mana‘o.
       She is not writing her opinion.
    4. ‘A‘ole pipi‘i loa ka mea ‘ai ma ka mokupuni ‘o Moloka‘i.
       Food on the island of Moloka‘i is not very expensive.
    5. ‘A‘ole e nīnau mau ana nā kamali‘i Hawai‘i.
       The Hawaiian children are not continually asking questions.

B. 1. ‘A‘ohe uila o Ni‘ihau.
    2. He ‘āina ho‘opulapula ko ko‘u kaikunāne.
    3. Nui nā waiho‘olu‘ulu‘u o ke ānuenue.
    4. ‘A‘ohe a‘u peni ‘ula‘ula.
    5. ‘Ekolu a ‘Ioli‘i mā kaikamahine.
    6. He kalaka hou ko ka ‘ohana.
    7. He mau manakō nui kā kākou.
    8. ‘Ehia wāwae o ka mo‘o?
    9. ‘Ehā ona wāwae.
   10. E ke kumu, nui kā mākou mau hō‘ike i kēia papa.
   11. Nui nā lio o ka haku Pukikī.
   12. He mau hua makekemia kā ka ‘iole.
   13. Nui nā ‘opihi o Keaukaha.
   14. He ka‘a ‘ele‘ele ko kēlā māka‘i.
   15. ‘A‘ohe pahu hau o ko‘u ke‘ena.

47

C. 1. 'Umikūmāiwa kanakolukūmāwalu
    2. Iwakāluakūmāono
    3. 'Umikūmākahi
    4. 'Ekolu hanele kanaonokūmālua
    5. 'Elima kaukani 'elua hanele kanahikukūmāhā
    6. 1898
    7. 57
    8. 23
    9. 90
   10. 649

D. 1. E ho'olimalima ana ka luahine i kēnā hale ia'u.
    2. Ua helu nā keiki me a'u i ka 'ōlelo Hawai'i.
    3. Ua ho'olohe 'oukou i ka lipine mai a'u?
    4. E ne'e paha mai ana ko'u 'anakala mai Hilo mai e noho me
       a'u.
    5. E ha'i mai kou mana'o ia'u, a e ha'i aku au i ko'u mana'o iā
       'oe.

E. 1. E kōkua a'e nō ho'i au iā 'oe.
    2. 'A'ohe ki'i'oni'oni ma Lāna'i i kēia manawa.
    3. 'A'ohe kīwī ma Hilo i ku'u wā kamali'i.
    4. E noho ana kou mau mākua ma ka mokupuni hea?
    5. 'O kou lā hānau 'ehia kēia?
    6. Aia ka limu kohu maika'i ma kēlā wahi wale nō.
    7. Hū ka nui o ka 'ulu ma ka mokupuni 'o Hawai'i.
    8. E a'o mai mākou i nā huahelu Hawai'i i kēia hopena pule.
    9. Emi loa ko'u kāma'a 'ula'ula hou.
   10. Ua kū'ai mai 'o Tūtū i ho'okahi kālani 'opihi wale nō no ka
       mea, ua pipi'i loa.

13

HAʻAWINA ʻUMIKŪMĀKOLU

I. TOPICS

A. *Ke* verb *nei* sentences
B. Locatives
C. *Mua* and *hope*
D. Verbless negative sentences
E. *Kēlā ʻano* X

II. BASIC SENTENCE TARGETS

1. *I loko*
2. *Ma mua* with time
3. *Ma luna*
4. *Ke* verb *nei*
5. Negative simple sentence; *kēia ʻano* X
6. *Mua* as adverb
7. Locative with directional
8. *Ma hope* with time
9. *Ma mua* with time

III. DIALOGS

1. At Lilinoe's restaurant

Lilinoe: Kimo, come inside the restaurant. There's a lot of rain this morning.
Kimo: I'm waiting for Lopaka.
Lilinoe: No problem. He'll come inside to look for you.

Kimo: Thanks. I'll drink coffee and read the newspaper before breakfast.

Lilinoe: Yes, good. The newspaper is on top of the table. I'm preparing the food, but the rice isn't cooked. Ten minutes maybe and (it will be) cooked.

Kimo: How about it? Is the coffee ready?

Lilinoe: Yeah, it's ready. It's over there, on top of the stove. There's milk inside the refrigerator.

Kimo: Thanks. Shucks, there's no sugar inside this bowl.

Lilinoe: There's a new bag under the table.

Kimo: Right, got it. I'll fill all the bowls.

Lilinoe: Thanks. Oh, here's Lopaka. Let's eat together!

Kimo: Can't. We're going to pick up my new car. Afterwards, we'll come back to eat.

Lilinoe: Okay. Bye.

2. At Lilinoe's restaurant (she's teaching the new waiter)

Lilinoe: Please, set the tables.

Waiter: Okay, but I'm Chinese. I'm not used to this kind of job.

Lilinoe: No problem. I'll show you.

Waiter: I'm putting the spoon and the fork on top of the plate. That's right, isn't it?

Lilinoe: No! Put the fork on top of the napkin on the left side of the plate.

Waiter: And what about the spoon and the knife? Leave them in the glass?

Lilinoe: No way! The spoon is on the right side of the plate, and put the knife between the plate and the spoon.

Waiter: And put the glass in front of the knife?

Lilinoe: Yes, that's right. Fill the sugar, the salt, and the shoyu, and the table will be ready.

3. Kimo and Lopaka return to the restaurant

Kimo: Hey, Lilinoe, Lopaka and I have returned.

Lilinoe: Good, the rice is ready. What do you want?

Kimo: I want two eggs on top of the rice.

Lilinoe: That's so delicious with shoyu. I'm frying Portuguese sausage. Do you want some too?

Kimo: Yes. And Lopaka only wants fruit juice and coffee.

Lilinoe: Why? Isn't he hungry?

Kimo: No. He already ate at home.

4. In Kimo's yard

Lehua: Uncle Kimo, come outside of the house quickly!
Kimo: Why? What's the trouble, Lehua?
Lehua: My kitten is climbing on top of the mango tree.
Kimo: No problem. Cats are used to that kind of activity.
Lehua: No. Climb up and get him.
Kimo: No way! Afterwards, he'll come back down.
Lehua: But he's afraid of that big dog over there.
Kimo: Ho! I didn't see him. Tsā! Get out of the yard!
Lehua: You're right, Uncle. The cat's coming back down. I'll take him inside the house.

IV. ANSWERS

A. Read this letter from Tuti to her family on Niʻihau.

Greetings, my dear family!

I am writing to let you know my doings here in Honolulu. I am staying at the Pagoda Hotel inland of the Ala Moana center. This shopping center is between Kapiʻolani Boulevard and Ala Moana Boulevard. Ala Moana Park is seaward of the boulevard.

Wow, there are so many expensive stores in Ala Moana. I just stand outside and look inside the windows. I'm afraid to go inside the stores because I don't have a lot of money, and I'm embarrassed to just look at everything. But I go into the Food Court to eat lunch. I stand among the food from everywhere, and I want to eat everything.

I'll be going back to Kauaʻi next month after my work at the University of Hawaii. Please write to me before then because I want to read the news on Niʻihau.

You all take care.

I am yours with affection,
Tuti

B. Write this letter in Hawaiian.

Aloha kākou, e kuʻu ʻohana!

Ke kākau nei au i kēia leka iā oukou e hōʻike i kaʻu mau hana i kēia mau lā. Ke noho nei māua ʻo Mealani i Hale Laulima ma kai o ke ala nui Dole. Ke noho nei nō hoʻi nā kāne i kēia hale noho haumana, akā ʻaʻole i nā lumi me nā wāhine! I kēlā lā, kēia lā, kūʻai mai au i ka ʻaina

kakahiaka ma ka hale 'aina 'o Hamilton ma hope o ka'u papa mua.
Noho au ma waho o Moore Hall a heluhelu a'e i ka nūpepa. Ma hope
iho, hele au i loko e ho'olohe i nā lipine Hawai'i. Ho'opa'a ha'awina nō
ho'i au ma waena o ka'u mau papa. Ma mua o ka 'aina ahiahi, hele iho
au i Cooke Field e holo. 'A'ole au holo 'āwīwī loa, akā he hana ho'ona-
nea ia. I ke ahiahi ma hope o ka 'aina ahiahi, hana au i kēlā me kēia
mea a ho'opa'a ha'awina. Nui loa ka'u mau ha'awina.

E 'olu'olu 'oukou , e kākau mai ia'u. Makemake au i nā ki'i o 'oukou
a me ku'u 'īlio. E mālama pono 'oukou.

'O wau iho nō me ke aloha,
Tuti

C.   1. Ke waiho nei au i nā manakō i loko o ka pahu hau.
     2. Ke 'imi nei ke kuene i ke koiū.
     3. E waiho i nā hua moa ma luna o ke kapuahi.
     4. Ke pi'i a'e nei nā mo'o i luna o ka puka aniani.
     5. Ke hiamoe iho nei nā 'īlio moloā ma lalo o ke kumu manakō.
     6. 'A'ohe o'u pōloli.
        'A'ole au pōloli.
     7. 'A'ohe o lākou hilahila.
        'A'ole lākou hilahila.
     8. 'A'ohe ona heluhelu i ka nūpepa.
        'A'ole 'o ia heluhelu i ka nūpepa.
     9. 'A'ohe o'u hana i kēia mahina.
        'A'ole au hana i kēia mahina.
    10. 'A'ohe wai hua'ai i loko o kēlā kī'aha.
    11. E hā'awi aku i ka waiū i ka pōpoki i loko o kēia ipu.
    12. E kau i ke puna i loko o ka ipu kōpa'a.
    13. 'A'ole makemake nā Pākē i kēlā 'ano laiki.
    14. 'A'ole 'ono loa kēia 'ano manakō.
    15. Maka'u mākou e 'ai i kēlā 'ano moa.

14

HAʻAWINA ʻUMIKŪMĀHĀ

I. TOPICS

A. Locatives with *o ʻu, ou, ona*
B. Comparative sentences
C. Negative imperatives
D. Medial *e* verb *ana*

II. BASIC SENTENCE TARGETS

1. Comparative sentence
2. Comparative sentence with possessive pronoun *(ou)*
3. Negative imperative sentence
4. Comparative sentence with *maikaʻi* omitted
5. Medial *e* verb *ana* sentence
6. Locative sentence with *ona*
7. Transitive verb sentence with *hoʻihoʻi*

III. DIALOGS

1. At Pua's house

Kale: Pua, don't leave the hot pot on the table.
Pua: Yes, I'll put the pot on top of the stove.
Kale: What's the stuff in that pot?
Pua: Only rice. I want eggs on top of hot rice with shoyu.
Kale: In my opinion, poi is more delicious than rice.
Pua: I eat poi with sugar and milk.
Kale: When I was a kid, I ate that kind of poi.
Pua: And what about now?
Kale: No. Poi with ʻopihi is better than poi with sugar.
Pua: I don't enjoy ʻopihi.
Kale: You're really lucky, because ʻopihi is really expensive nowadays.

53

2. At Lilinoe's restaurant

Kimo: Lilinoe, look outside of the window. My new car is in front of
           the restaurant.
Lilinoe: Ho, the pretty! This new car is bigger than the previous car,
           isn't it?
Kimo: Yeah, and it's more expensive too!
Lilinoe: No problem. Drink your coffee!
Kimo: Where's the sugar?
Lilinoe: "Blind eye," it's in the bowl in front of you!
Kimo: Don't pick on me! My eyesight is better than yours.
Lilinoe: That's true maybe, but I can still see that cop putting a ticket
           on top of your car.
Kimo: Oh my goodness! Why?
Lilinoe: Because that place is forbidden.
Kimo: You didn't tell me!
Lilinoe: You didn't ask me!

3. At Luika's house in Honolulu

Luika: Pua, look at these pictures of Kimo "folks."
Pua: Ho, the big that car in back of him!
Luika: That's his new car. He's really happy.
Pua: A big car is a good thing, because his family is rather large.
Luika: Yes, and they always go to Hilo.
Pua: Maybe a truck is better than a car.
Luika: Maybe not, because there's a lot of rain in Hilo.
Pua: Who's this girl in the middle of the picture?
Luika: That's the youngest, Lieka.
Pua: She's so tall! I want to show the pictures to Kale.
Luika: Okay, but don't forget to return them!
Pua: I won't forget.

4. At Lilinoe's restaurant

Waiter: Lilinoe, there's a big gecko on top of the window.
Lilinoe: Don't be afraid. He won't eat you.
Waiter: Don't tease me. I've been afraid of geckoes since I was a kid.
Lilinoe: Really? My kid sister really likes geckoes. She leaves water in
           a small glass, and they come to drink.
Waiter: And what, maybe she gives them food?
Lilinoe: Yes, she puts guava jelly on a very small plate.
Waiter: Wow, maybe she's kind of crazy.

Lilinoe: Hey, don't talk like that! She's smarter than you.
Waiter: Maybe not. What does she do?
Lilinoe: She's a Hawaiian language teacher at the University of Hawaii.
Waiter: Tsā, I'm right. She's kind of crazy.

IV. ANSWERS

A. 1. 'Oi aku ka pipi'i o ke kāwele lole ma mua o ke kāwele pepa.
  2. 'Oi aku ka nui o kona maka ma mua o kona'ōpū.
  3. 'Oi aku ka 'ono o ka pua'a ma mua o ka pipi.
  4. 'Oi aku ke akamai o ka pōpoki ma mua o ka 'īlio.
  5. 'Oi aku ka hilahila o kāna wahine ma mua ona.
  6. 'Oi aku ke kapuahi ea ma mua o ke kapuahi uila.
  7. 'Oi aku paha kou pōloli ma mua o'u.
  8. 'Oi aku ka maka'u o ka mo'o ma mua ou.
  9. 'Oi aku ka nani o kēia kī'aha ma mua o kēlā.
  10. 'Oi aku ka nui o nā nūpepa haole ma mua o nā nūpepa Kepanī.
  11. 'Oi aku ke anu o Waimea ma mua o Kawaihae.
  12. 'Oi aku ke akamai o ka 'aihue ma mua o ka māka'i.
  13. 'Oi aku ka 'ono o ka i'a ma mua o ka pipi.
  14. 'Oi aku ka nani o kēia lei haku ma mua o ka lei wili.
  15. 'Oi aku ka nui o ko ka 'īlio po'o ma mua o ka 'iole.
  16. 'Oi aku ka mālie o ke kai o Ka'a'awa ma mua o Pūpūkea.
  17. 'Oi aku ka nīele o nā keiki haole ma mua o nā keiki Hawai'i.
  18. 'Oi aku ka wīwī o Sissy Spacek ma mua o Bo Derek.
  19. 'Oi aku ke kolohe o nā luāhine ma mua o nā kaikamāhine.
  20. 'Oi aku ka pipi'i o ka hale 'aina 'o Michel's ma mua o McDonald's.

B. 'Eleu: E ke kuene, e ho'iho'i aku 'oe i kēia moa; 'a'ole mo'a.
  Waiter: Hiki nō; e hō'ike a'e au i ka haku.
  Ha'aheo: Mai hana 'ino aku 'oe iā ia!
  'Eleu: 'A'ole au e hana 'ino ana, akā, 'a'ohe o'u makemake i ka moa maka.
  Ha'aheo: 'A'ole maka loa. 'O ia ke 'ano Pākē.
  'Eleu: 'Oi aku ke 'ano haole me mua o ke 'ano Pākē.
  Ha'aheo: Inā pēlā, mai hele 'oe i ka hale 'aina Pākē. Aia 'o Kentucky Fried Chicken ma'ō, ma kēlā 'ao'ao o ke ala nui.

15

HAʻAWINA ʻUMIKŪMĀLIMA

I. TOPICS

A. Verb classes
B. Stative verbs with causatives

II. BASIC SENTENCE TARGETS

1. Intransitive verb sentence with *hoʻi*
2. Transitive verb sentence with *hoʻihoʻi*
3. Transitive verb sentence with *hōʻauʻau*
4. Stative verb sentence with *hāmama*
5. Transitive verb sentence with *wehe*
6. Stative verb sentence with *paʻa*
7. Transitive verb sentence with *pani*
8. Transitive verb sentence with *hūnā*
9. Intransitive verb sentence with *peʻe*
10. Stative verb sentence with causative
11. Stative verb sentence with causative
12. Stative verb sentence with causative

III. DIALOGS

1. On the telephone in Hawaiʻi

Kimo: Lilinoe, Lauaʻe and I are returning to Hilo tomorrow.
Lilinoe: Good; I'm always happy to see you two. Perhaps you have something to do here?
Kimo: Yes, I'm returning the new car.

Lilinoe: Goodness! Why? A big problem?

Kimo: The back doors are stuck. We try to open the doors but cannot.

Lilinoe: Tsā! That's a waste of time. Is that the only problem?

Kimo: No. We want to close the windows, but cannot. (They're) still open!

Lilinoe: No problem; there isn't a lot of rain in Kona.

Kimo: Hey, don't make fun of me. This is a new car, and expensive too.

Lilinoe: Yeah, right; will they fix the car?

Kimo: I don't want this car. I'm going to ask them to return my money.

2. At Lilinoe's house

Kimo: Halloo, Lilinoe, here we are!

Laua'e: She's not answering.

Kimo: Yeah, all the doors are closed. Maybe she went to the store.

Laua'e: No problem. We'll just wait.

Kimo: She didn't close the windows. I'll climb inside the open window and open the door.

Laua'e: No way! Let's look for the key. Maybe she hid the key outside of the house.

Kimo: Yeah, you're right. I forgot; there's a key inside of this flower pot.

Laua'e: Good. We'll open the door and return the key.

3. At Pua's house

Luika: Pua, you guys have a new dog.

Pua: Yes; Koko was killed by a car.

Luika: Too bad! A real pity! And what's this kind of dog?

Pua: He's a white shepherd. This kind of dog is famous for being good-hearted.

Luika: Yes, and he's beautiful too. But there are a lot of fleas on him.

Pua: For real? Wow, I'll bathe him with flea soap.

Luika: Yes, because it's a big problem if the fleas go inside the house.

Pua: Yeah, yeah. Flea bites are really itchy.

Luika: Yes, but the itching is relieved with raw papaya.

Pua: Really? I never heard that before.

Luika: Yes, it's a soothing substance for all bites.

4. At the university in Mānoa

Nīele: Pua, how's work at the university?

Pua: I'm kind of tired of this kind of work.

Nīele: What? Are the students no good?

Pua: No, no; they're good, and nice too; but nevertheless they are famous for laziness!

Nīele: I've heard the teachers are lazier.

Pua: Hey, don't abuse (us). We work continually night and day.

Nīele: Tsā, that's the trouble! Don't work all the time! Go out to Mānoa Gardens after class.

Pua: Maybe (that's) right. I'll go drink with my students; that might be a relaxing pastime.

Nīele: Yes, and your tiredness will be ended in relaxation.

5. In the Hawaiian language class

Teacher: Hopoe, where's ʻEleu?

Hopoe: He's hiding outside of the door.

Teacher: Why? Is he embarrassed?

Hopoe: Yes. He doesn't want to dance.

Teacher: Tsā! ʻEleu, come inside and dance with us.

ʻEleu: No. I'm really embarrassed. I'm not used to this kind of activity.

Teacher: Us too! But, let's try! That's the main thing.

Hopoe: Yes. The ancestors said this saying: "Dare to dance; leave embarrassment at home."

ʻEleu: What's the meaning of this saying?

Teacher: Here's the meaning: don't be afraid to try new things.

ʻEleu: Yeah, that's right. Let's dance!

IV. ANSWERS

A.   The doors of our church are open day and night. We don't close the doors because people might want to come inside at any time. The youngsters come before and after school, and they sit on the porch because there is a lot of rain in Kahaluʻu. They take good care of the church; they don't mistreat it with graffiti.

Yesterday a very small kitten came into the church. I tried to catch it, but it ran very fast and hid behind the organ. Too bad, it was so afraid of me. Afterwards, it emerged and ran outside and climbed up on top of a very tall coconut tree. It didn't come back down. Day and night it stayed put and cried. This morning a policeman came to help, and he looked for the kitten hiding above him. But his eyesight isn't good. The kitten's eyesight is better than his, and it didn't come out. The policeman went back to the police station. After that, the kitten came back down, because it was very hungry. All the neighbors were really happy.

B. 1. The door was closed by the wind.
    2. The house was consumed by the fire.
    3. My hands are itchy on account of the mango leaves.
    4. Hilo is famous for heavy rain.
    5. Your face is relaxed by the beer drinking.
    6. Ua kaulana 'o Kaua'i i ka hē'ī.
    7. Ua 'eha ko'u lima i ka wai wela.
    8. Ua nuha nā haumana i ka ha'awina nui.
    9. Ua māluhiluhi ka makuahine i ka hana kolohe a kāna keiki.
    10. Ua huhū ke kuene i ka hana 'ino.
    11. Ua make ka manu i ka pōpoki pōloli.

C. 1. My older sister is bringing back my children after school.
    2. My husband will bathe the dogs.
    3. The rats are hiding under the stove.
    4. Hide the dessert inside the icebox.
    5. Haoles bathe in the morning, but Hawaiians like to bathe in the evening before sleeping.
    6. Mai poina e ho'i mai i ka hale i kēia ahiahi.
    7. Ua ho'iho'i mai 'o Kamohoali'i i ke kalaka ma hope o ka hana.
    8. Ua pe'e 'o Kamapua'a ma lalo o ke kalo ma Kaluanui.
    9. Mai poina e hūnā i ke kī ma waho o ka hale.
    10. Ke ho'iho'i nei au i kēia ka'a no ka mea, ua make ia i ka hele mua.

REVIEW 4
HOʻI HOPE ʻEHĀ

I. ANSWERS

A.   1. ʻOi aku ka ikaika o ko Russ Francis makua kāne ma mua ona.
       ʻOi aku ka ikaika o ka makua kāne o Russ Francis ma mua ona.
    2. ʻOi aku ka waiwai o Hiram Fong ma mua ou.
       ʻOi aku ko Hiram Fong waiwai ma mua ou.
    3. ʻOi aku ka momona o ko Kaleo makuahine ma mua o koʻu makuahine.
    4. ʻOi aku ka moloā o kaʻu mau haumana ma mua oʻu.
    5. ʻOi aku ka māʻona o ka mea ʻai Hawaiʻi ma mua o ka mea ʻai Kepanī.

B.   1. ma lalo o ka nūpepa; i lalo o ka nūpepa
    2. ma luna o ka laiki; i luna o ka nūpepa
    3. ma mua ona; i mua ona
    4. ma hope oʻu; i hope oʻu
    5. ma loko ou; i loko ou
    6. ma hope o kākou
    7. ma waho o ka puka; i waho o ka puka
    8. ma uka o ka hale pule; i uka o ka hale pule
    9. ma kai o ke ala nui; i kai o ke ala nui
   10. ma ka ʻaoʻao ʻākau o ka pākaukau; i ka ʻaoʻao ʻākau o ka pākaukau
   11. E piʻi aʻe ana kāu popoki i luna o ke kaʻa.
   12. Aia ka puke ma mua ou.
   13. Aia ʻo Māmā i loko o ka hale e palai ana i ka moa.
   14. Ua ʻai mua mākou.
   15. E hiki mai ana lākou ma hope o ka ʻaina ahiahi.

C. 1. My stomach is full from eating mango.
   2. Tūtū is mad at me.
   3. The mother is tired from the hard work.
   4. Kamehameha I was famous for intelligence.
   5. We are used to that kind of activity.
   6. Ua mau ke ea o ka 'āina i ka pono.
   7. Ua make ka wahine i kāna kāne pupule.
   8. Ua hilahila nā kaikamāhine i ka hana kolohe a nā keiki kāne.
   9. Ua pōmaika'i kākou i ke aloha.
   10. Ua maka'u nā manu i ka pōpoki pōloli.

D. 1. 'A'ole 'olua i ho'olohe pono i ke kumu.
   2. Ua lohe au i ka helu kelepona o ka hale kū'ai ma ke kīwī.
   3. E hapai ana nā keiki i nā pū'olo kaumaha.
   4. Ho'opa'a ha'awina mākou i ka hopena pule apau.
   5. Ua kama'āina 'oe i nā kānaka e ne'e mai ana?
   6. E ho'opiha i nā kī'aha apau me ka waiū.
   7. E ho'iho'i aku ana ke kuene i nā hua moa maka.
   8. Mai 'au'au kai ma hope o ka 'aina awakea.
   9. Mai ho'iho'i aku i kēlā 'ano kini.
   10. 'A'ohe o'u makemake i kēlā 'ano koiū.

16

HAʻAWINA ʻUMIKŪMĀONO

I. TOPICS

A. Passive voice sentences
B. *Kekahi*
C. *Mau* with *ʻaʻohe* and numbers
D. Word order in verb phrases

II. BASIC SENTENCE TARGETS

1. *Ua* passive sentence with common noun agent
2. *Ua* passive sentence with proper noun agent
3. *Ua* passive sentence with pronoun agent *(e ia)*
4. *Ua* passive sentence with pronoun agent *(e aʻu)*
5. *Ua* passive sentence with *paha*
6. Negative completed action passive sentence
7. *Ke* verb *nei* passive sentence
8. *E* verb *ana* passive sentence with *mai* (word order)
9. *E* verb *ana* passive sentence with *nō* (word order)
10. *Kekahi* X *ʻē a ʻe*
11. *Kekahi i kekahi*
12. *ʻAʻohe* with *mau*
13. Numbers with *mau*

III. DIALOGS

1. At Lilinoe's restaurant

Lilinoe: Oh goodness! I'm so tired this morning.
Waiter: If that's the case, go back home. There isn't a lot of work here.
Lilinoe: Is the rice cooked?
Waiter: Yes, and all the dishes are being prepared by the new waiter.
Lilinoe: Really? Is he trained in this kind of work?
Waiter: Yes, he was taught by his mother. His mother was taken to Hong Kong as a child. He is very familiar with all kinds of Chinese food.
Lilinoe: If that's the case, I'm going back. Kimo "folks" are at home.
Waiter: Give them my regards. Goodbye, and take care of yourself.
Lilinoe: Yes, goodbye until tomorrow.

2. Lilinoe returns home

Lilinoe: Wow, the whole house has been cleaned. What are you doing, Lauaʻe?
Lauaʻe: I'm waiting for Kimo, so I'm just doing this and that.
Lilinoe: Ho, the dishes and clothes are washed too! Thanks a lot!
Lauaʻe: It's my pleasure. You have a lot of work at the restaurant; there isn't enough time to work at home too.
Lilinoe: Yes, that's right. But where's Kimo? Is he returning the new car to the car dealer?
Lauaʻe: No; the car was returned by him yesterday. But the money wasn't returned.
Lilinoe: Is he getting the money?
Lauaʻe: Yes, he was taken by Lopaka.
Lilinoe: Are they coming back to eat lunch?
Lauaʻe: Yes; I called the restaurant, and a pizza is being delivered.
Lilinoe: You're so smart! I love pizza with beer.
Lauaʻe: Me too! And here they are and the pizza too!

3. On the telephone

Lilinoe: Pua, have you heard the news? Kimo's truck was stolen last night.
Pua: Oh my goodness! He has so many problems! He doesn't have any cars, does he?

Lilinoe: Yes. His new car was returned to the dealer. He hasn't
           bought another car.
Pua: How about it? Perhaps the thief was seen by the neighbors?
Lilinoe: Yes, and he is being sought by the police in Kona.
Pua: So what? Did Kimo "folks" go back to Kona on the bus?
Lilinoe: No way! ʻAlapaki loaned them his car.
Pua: Our family is really blessed, aren't we? We always help each
           other.
Lilinoe: Yes, we are truly blessed with love.

4. At the university

Tuti: Pua, is the new lesson written?
Pua: Yes, it's ready. Are you making a tape today?
Tuti: Yes, two hours have been reserved in the recording room.
Pua: One hour is probably enough. This lesson isn't long.
Tuti: I'm being helped by Kanaʻi.
Pua: That's good; his voice is greatly admired by the students.
Tuti: I'll go make some copies of the lesson.
Pua: Oh, I forgot. Here are the copies. They have already been made
        by me.
Tuti: Good; I'll go meet Kanaʻi.

IV. ANSWERS

A.   "The Lazy Beauty"

One day, two girls went to dig sweet potatoes. Afterwards, they
took their sweet potatoes under a pūhala tree. They started to broil
the sweet potatoes, but the lover of one of them arrived. The girl
and her boyfriend climbed on top of the pūhala tree to make love.
From time to time, the girl on top of the pūhala called to the girl
below, "Hey, turn my sweet potato." "Yes," answered the girl
below, and she turned her own sweet potato. She didn't look at the
sweet potato of the girl up above. And when one sweet potato was
cooked, she ate it and broiled another sweet potato again. The girl
above called again, "Turn my sweet potato." The girl below
agreed, but she didn't cook those sweet potatoes. She ate all of her
sweet potatoes and went to swim. The girl above remembered her
sweet potatoes and called again, "Hey you, turn my sweet potatoes." No answer. She called again in a loud voice, "Turn my sweet
potatoes!" No answer. They came down and saw the sweet potato

burned to a crisp in the fire. The lazy girl was really mad. The girl came back from swimming, and the lazy one abused her. She answered, "No lazy beauties for Ka'ū!" And with these words, she stood up and left with her friend's lover. That guy knew that if the lazy beauty were his wife, his sweet potatoes would always be burned in the fire.

Nowadays, the parents of Ka'ū tell their lazy daughters, "No lazy beauties for Ka'ū!" Here's the meaning of this proverb: the young men of Ka'ū don't want lazy girlfriends! A beautiful face and body are not enough, because the men want to eat delicious food, not burnt sweet potatoes.

B. 1. Makemake au i ke kele 'ē a'e.
    2. Ua ho'oipoipo kekahi kaikamahine, a ua pūlehu kekahi i ka 'uala.
    3. E holoi ana kekahi keiki i nā pā, a e kāwele ana kekahi.
    4. I kekahi lā, e ho'onanea ana ka papa i ka pā'ina.
    5. Ke kōkua a'e nei nā 'ōpio kekahi i kekahi.
    6. Ho'ohenehene mau 'o 'Alena lāua 'o Hepualei kekahi i kekahi.
    7. Ke 'imi nei au i kekahi kumu 'ōlelo Hawai'i 'ē a'e; hana 'ino mau 'o Pua iā mākou.
    8. E ho'iho'i 'ia ana mai kekahi mau mea e ka 'aihue.
    9. Ua poina ke kahuhipa i kekahi mau hipa i waho, a ua nahu 'ia lākou e ka 'īlio i ka pō nei.
   10. Ua lawa kekahi kope 'ē a'e.

C. 1. 'Elua o'u mau mākua e ola mau ana.
    2. 'A'ohe ona mau kūpuna ma Hawai'i nei.
    3. 'A'ole i pau ka hō'ike ma hope o 'elua mau hola.
    4. 'A'ohe a kākou mau hē'ī maka, 'a'ole anei?
    5. Aia 'ehā mau manakō maka i loko o kēia 'eke pepa.

D. 1. Ua 'ike 'ia nō ka 'aihue e nā hoa noho.
    2. Ke kākau 'ia nei ka puke 'ōlelo Hawai'i hou e a'u.
    3. Ua kuke pono 'ia kēia mau hua moa e Māmā.
    4. Ua 'ai 'ia ke kele kuawa apau e nā mo'o.
    5. E ho'onoho paha 'ia a'e ana ka pākaukau e lāua.
    6. Ua hā'awi 'ia mai ka helu kelepona ia'u e ia.
    7. E ho'iho'i paha 'ia mai ana ko Lia kalaka.
    8. Ua 'ae 'ia mai kēia ka'a ia'u e ko'u kaikua'ana.
    9. Auē! Ua 'aihue 'ia aku ka na'aukake e ka 'īlio pōloli.
   10. E pani 'ia ana nā puka aniani a me nā puka e mākou ma hope o ka papa hope loa.

E. 1. Ke wehe ʻia aʻe nei ka puka e aʻu.
       The door is being opened by me.
    2. E heluhelu ʻia aʻe ana ka pepa e ia.
       The paper will be read by her.
    3. Ua ʻai ʻia ka poi apau e ʻoe?
       Was all the poi eaten by you?
    4. Ua pani ʻia aku nā puka e ke kumu.
       The doors were closed by the teacher.
    5. E lawe ʻia mai ana kēlā me kēia mea ʻono mai Hilo mai e kou
       hoahānau.
       Various goodies will be brought from Hilo by your cousin.
    6. E ʻai ʻia ana ka laulau e Lono.
       The laulau will be eaten by Lono.
    7. Ke heluhelu ʻia nei ka pepa e ke kauka.
       The paper is being read by the doctor.
    8. Ke pani ʻia nei ka puka aniani e ia.
       The window is being closed by him.
    9. E lawe ʻia mai ana nā makana e lāua.
       The presents will be brought by them.
   10. Ke hāʻawi ʻia aku nei ka leka iā Kala e ʻIokimo.
       The letter is being given to Kala by ʻIokimo.
   11. Ua holoi ʻia ka lole e ia.
       The clothes were washed by him.
   12. E ʻike ʻia mai ana mākou e koʻu makuahine.
       We will be seen by my mother.

17
HAʻAWINA UMIKŪMĀHIKU

I. TOPICS

A. *Hiki* sentences
B. *Inā* with pronouns
C. N-possessives

II. BASIC SENTENCE TARGETS

1. *Hiki* sentence
2. Negative *hiki* sentence
3. *Hiki* with *nō* and *iaʻu*
4. *Hiki* with compound object
5. Idiom
6. Idiom
7. *Inā* with pronoun
8. N-possessive
9. N-possessive

III. DIALOGS

1. At Lilinoe's restaurant

ʻAlapaki: Lilinoe, is everything ready for the lūʻau this weekend?
Lilinoe: No way! And Uncle Pila "folks" are really worried.
ʻAlapaki: This is his "how many" birthday?
Lilinoe: His ninetieth birthday. He was born in 1898.
ʻAlapaki: Wow, how old! But his health is still good.

Lilinoe: And what about the imu? Are you guys cooking the pig on Friday?

ʻAlapaki: No. I'm picking up the pig from Honokaʻa on Friday, and we're cooking on Saturday. So we can't help you with the other food.

Lilinoe: Oh my goodness! That's a big problem! The lūʻau and the squid haven't been cooked; the chicken hasn't been cut up; the coconut milk hasn't been prepared. There's a lot of work.

ʻAlapaki: Maybe Lauaʻe and ʻEkekela can help you.

Lilinoe: They can't get off work.

ʻAlapaki: How about Luika "guys"? Maybe they can come from Honolulu before the weekend.

Lilinoe: It might be possible. I'll call them right away. But this is really frustrating.

ʻAlapaki: Yeah, right, but it can't be helped. I can't pick up the pig before Friday.

Lilinoe: True, and you're forgiven this time. But don't do it again!

2. On the telephone on Thursday afternoon

Lilinoe: Pua, can you possibly come back to Hilo this evening?

Pua: This evening? Why? I have two classes tomorrow.

Lilinoe: Because there's a lot of work for the lūʻau on Saturday, and ʻAlapaki "guys" can't help me.

Pua: What? Can't the young folks help you?

Lilinoe: Yes, they can, but they're not very used to this kind of activity.

Pua: Did you talk to Luika? Maybe she can go?

Lilinoe: I already asked her, and she is coming. It would be a good thing if the two of you came together.

Pua: Tsā! Maybe Tuti can teach my classes. I'll call her.

3. On the phone in Honolulu

Pua: Hi, Tuti. Can I possibly bother you?

Tuti: Sure can. What do you want?

Pua: My older sister asked me to go to Hilo right away, but I have some classes tomorrow.

Tuti: No problem. I can teach the classes. It's a pleasure for me.

Pua: Excuse me for this burden on you.

Tuti: No big deal. It can't be helped. You go help your family. That's
           the main thing.
Pua: Thanks a lot, Tuti. You are really a good friend.
Tuti: No, the pleasure is mine. Give my aloha to the family in Hilo.

4. At the university

Piʻilani: Tuti, we can't do the exam next Monday.
Tuti: Why? This is only Friday. You guys can study all weekend.
Piʻilani: No, no. Here's the problem. We have some questions about
           the lesson, but Pua didn't come. So we can't ask her.
Tuti: It can't be helped. You can ask me today.
Piʻilani: Wow, Tuti. We're really worried about this big exam.
Tuti: Tsā! Exams are a common occurrence in this class. No big
           deal! Let's start the class.
Piʻilani: No; let's go eat together in the restaurant and practice the
           Hawaiian language.
Tuti: Yes, that's a good activity. After class we can go.

IV. ANSWERS

A. "The First Breadfruit Tree"

In ancient times, a god arrived from Kahiki and lived in Hawaiʻi.
His name was Kū. He married a Hawaiian woman, and they had a
lot of children. The woman did not know that her husband was a
god because he worked at everything like the other men.

At one time, the rain didn't rain for a very long time. The taro
and the sweet potato and all the crops died. There wasn't enough
food, and Kū and his family were very hungry. Kū looked at his
wife and children, and his pity for them was very great. So one day
he told his dearly beloved wife, "My beloved wife, I can get food for
you all, but if I go I can't come back." His wife didn't agree to this
action, but later she heard the crying voices of the children, and she
asked her husband to go and get food for them.

The entire family went into the yard, and they expressed their
love to each other. Kū said to his family, "I'm going to stand on my
head and dig down underneath the dirt. Afterwards, food will
emerge. Aloha!" And he stood on his head and disappeared.

His wife sat down at that place, and she cried night and day.
After several days, a shoot emerged. This tree grew very quickly,
and the family ate the fruit. This was Hawaiʻi's first breadfruit tree.

Only Kū's family could pick the breadfruit; the other people couldn't. If a person tried to pick, the tree returned under the ground.

But later, offspring emerged from the first tree, and these other trees were given to all the families to plant in their own gardens.

The breadfruit was given to the Hawaiian people by Kū, a sacrifice of love.

B.　1. Hiki iā ʻoe ke heʻe nalu? ʻAʻole, akā, hiki iaʻu ke ʻauʻau kai.
　　2. Hiki iā Kalau ke ʻōlelo Hawaiʻi? ʻAe, hiki i kona ʻohana apau.
　　3. Hiki iā ia ke hele i ke kikowaena kūʻai me kāua?
　　4. ʻAʻole hiki iā ia ke hele no ka mea, huhū loa kona makuahine iā ia.
　　5. Hiki i ka lawaiʻa ke kūʻai aku i kāna mau iʻa?
　　6. ʻAe, hiki iā ia, akā, makemake ʻo ia e hāʻawi wale.
　　7. Ua hiki iā lākou ke ʻike i nā waʻa?
　　8. ʻAʻole i hiki iā lākou ke ʻike.
　　9. Hiki i ka pōpoki ke piʻi aʻe i ke kumu lāʻau, akā, ʻaʻole hiki i ka ʻīlio.
　10. ʻAʻole hiki ke kanu i ka ʻulu ma Niʻihau, no ka mea, ʻaʻole lawa ka ua.

C.　1. Ua hiki iā Kū ke kiʻi i ka mea ʻai na kona ʻohana.
　　2. Inā ʻo ia i hele, ʻaʻole i hiki iā ia ke hoʻi mai.
　　3. Inā ʻoe makemake, e ʻako aʻe au i nā pua nāu.
　　4. Ua hana ʻia kēia lei poʻo noʻu e ʻAulani.
　　5. Ma hope o ka ua nui, e puka aʻe ana nā kupu i kēlā me kēia wahi i ka māla ʻai.
　　6. ʻAʻole hiki i ka ʻelemakule ke ʻalo i nā kaʻa ʻāwīwī.
　　7. E ke kuene, e lawe mai i ka laiki naʻu a me ka poi ʻulu na Tuti!
　　8. A mai poina i ka pipi kaula na māua!
　　9. ʻAʻole lawa ka pipi kaula na ʻolua.
　10. I ka wā kahiki, ua ʻeli ka poʻe o Niʻihau i ka lua nui a kanu i ke kumu lāʻau ʻulu i loko.

18

HAʻAWINA ʻUMIKŪMĀWALU

I. TOPICS

A. *Maopopo*
B. *Loaʻa*
C. N-possessive in initial position
D. N-possessive in final position

II. BASIC SENTENCE TARGETS

1. *Maopopo* sentence with noun
2. *Maopopo* sentence with pronoun
3. Negative *maopopo* sentence
4. *Loaʻa* sentence with pronoun
5. *Loaʻa* sentence with pronoun
6. Negative *loaʻa* sentence
7. *Ua loaʻa* sentence
8. *Loaʻa* sentence meaning "Is there any?"
9. Initial n-possessive sentence with *nāu*
10. Initial n-possessive sentence with *no kākou*
11. Initial n-possessive sentence with *noʻu*
12. Initial n-possessive sentence with *no wai*
13. Initial n-possessive sentence with *no*
14. *E* verb *ana* sentence with final n-possessive
15. Negative "have-a" sentence with final n-possessive
16. Simple sentence with final n-possessive
17. Stative sentence with final n-possessive

III. DIALOGS

1. At the university

Kanaʻi: Pua, does your whole family understand Hawaiian?

Pua: No, because my mother can't speak Hawaiian. We didn't speak Hawaiian at home.

Kanaʻi: But she's a Hawaiian woman, isn't she?

Pua: Yes, she's Hawaiian on her mother's side. But my grandmother was raised by a haole family.

Kanaʻi: And how about your father? Is he pure Hawaiian?

Pua: No, he's part Hawaiian, part Chinese. He can speak Chinese.

Kanaʻi: And you probably understand that kind of language?

Pua: No. He didn't speak Chinese to us. We only spoke English at home.

Kanaʻi: But you are proficient in Hawaiian now.

Pua: Yes, I learned it at the University of Hawaii.

Kanaʻi: Really? If that's so, maybe I can learn.

2. At the dormitory

Kalei: Hopoe, this new lesson is for you. You don't have it, do you?

Hopoe: Yes, I don't have it. I couldn't go to class today.

Kalei: Why? The teacher asked me, and I didn't know.

Hopoe: I got a letter from my aunty on Maui. She asked me to go right away and get something for her. So I didn't go to class.

Kalei: You are a lucky student because the teacher sent this lesson for you. There's a test about these things tomorrow.

Hopoe: But I don't understand these new things. Maybe I can trouble you?

Kalei: Maybe (you) can, maybe (you) can't. What's my reward?

Hopoe: Wow! Don't you have any aloha for me?

Kalei: Yes, there's aloha, but the aloha and the help will be greater if a reward is received.

Hopoe: Here's the payment. I'll clean your room for the rest of this semester.

Kalei: That's a good reward. I can certainly help you.

3. At Luika's house

Makia: Mama, are these new clothes for us?

Luika: Yes, (they) were sent by your Aunt Lilinoe.

Makia: We're really lucky, aren't we? And what? Are these jeans for me?

Luika: Yes, and the shirt too! We all got new clothes.

Makia: I don't understand the reason for all these gifts.

Luika: There's really pretty clothes in Hilo, and a reasonable price too. So she bought and sent them for us.

Makia: Who is the lauhala hat for?

Luika: That's for Papa. I'm making a peacock feather lei for him.

Makia: I want a feather lei for me.

Luika: Okay. I can teach you. But you start with chicken feathers. Start with that kind of inexpensive feather, and later you can make another lei with expensive feathers.

Makia: Good. Thanks, Mama. I'm really a lucky girl. I'm going to write a thank-you note to Aunty.

4. At Tamashiro market

Luika: Is there octopus this morning?

Clerk: The octopus is inside that basin.

Luika: Wow, it isn't dead!

Clerk: Yes, it's very fresh octopus!

Luika: I can't cook a live octopus.

Clerk: No problem. Bite it in between the eyes, and it will die.

Luika: Isn't there any dead octopus?

Clerk: Got, but this octopus is more tasty.

Luika: Do you know how to do this?

Clerk: Yes, I'm very used to biting octopus.

Luika: Perhaps you could bite the octopus for me?

Clerk: Cannot. If the Board of Health knew, there would be a lot of trouble for us.

Luika: If I leave the octopus inside the refrigerator, maybe he'll die.

Clerk: Yes, after a while, he would die.

IV. ANSWERS

A. 1. ʻAʻole maopopo iaʻu.
2. Maopopo kona inoa i kou makuahine?
3. Maopopo iā ʻoukou apau ka manaʻo o kēia hua ʻōlelo?
4. ʻAe, maopopo nō iā mākou.
5. ʻAʻole i hoʻolohe kekahi mau haumana, a ʻaʻole maopopo iā lākou.
6. Maopopo ka ʻōlelo Hawaiʻi i kuʻu tūtū.
7. ʻAʻole maopopo ka ʻōlelo Hawaiʻi i kuʻu tūtū no ka mea, he Kepanī ʻo ia.
8. Maopopo iā ia ka ʻōlelo Kepanī?
9. Maopopo nō iā ia.
10. I nehinei, ua hoʻokuʻu ʻia ka papa ʻōlelo Hawaiʻi no ka mea, ʻaʻole maopopo iā mākou ka haʻawina, a huhū ʻo Pua.
11. Maopopo paha iā mākou i kēia lā.

B. 1. Ua loaʻa ka ʻaihue i ka mākaʻi.
2. Ua loaʻa iā ʻoe kāu kālā?
3. E loaʻa ana nā puke i ke kumu.
4. Ua loaʻa ka heʻe i ka lawaiʻa.
5. Ua loaʻa ka manō ma ka makeke ʻo Tamashiro.
6. Loaʻa ka maile a me ka ʻawapuhi ma Panaʻewa.
7. ʻAʻole i loaʻa iaʻu ka haʻawina i ka Pōʻalima.
8. ʻAʻole pilikia; ua loaʻa iā Moana.
9. ʻAʻole e loaʻa ana ke kaʻa hou i koʻu kaikunāne no kona lā hānau.
10. Loaʻa nā kaikamāhine nani loa ma Hilo.

C. 1. Maopopo ka haʻawina i nā haumana.
2. Maopopo iaʻu kāna helu kelepona.
3. Maopopo ka manaʻo o kēia hua ʻōlelo iā Kaʻupena.
4. Ua maopopo ka hana kapa i ka poʻe kahiko.
5. Akā, ʻaʻole maopopo iā mākou i kēia mau lā.
6. Ua loaʻa iā ʻoe kāu mau puke?
7. E loaʻa ana iaʻu ke kālā?
8. Ua loaʻa ka nūhou i koʻu makuahine i ka pō nei.
9. Ua loaʻa iā ia ʻeono mau manakō.
10. E loaʻa ana kona kaʻa hou iā Ānuenue i kēia mahina aʻe.
11. Ua loaʻa kekahi mau ʻiole i ka pōpoki i kēia kakahiaka.
12. Ua loaʻa ka mea waiwai apau i ka ipo a ka ʻaihue.
13. Hiki iā ʻoe ke ʻae mai i kekahi mau puke iaʻu?

14. Hiki iā lākou ke hele ma hope o ka papa.
15. Hiki i nā haumana ke kū aʻe ma mua o ko lākou mau pākaukau kākau.
16. Hiki i koʻu mau kūpuna ke ʻōlelo Hawaiʻi.
17. Hiki iā Nāpua ke hoʻihoʻi i nā pepa.
18. ʻAʻole hiki iaʻu ke ʻai i ka iʻa.
19. ʻAʻole hiki iā ʻoukou ke hele mā luna o ke kaʻa.
20. ʻAʻole hiki i kā lāua mau keiki ke noho mālie.

D.   1. No wai kēia lei hulu pīkake?
     2. Ua hana au (i ka lei) no ka ʻelemakule.
     3. Nona nō hoʻi kēia pāpale lauhala?
     4. Nona kēia mau lole hou apau.
     5. Na ke ʻīlio ke koena?
     6. Na ke ʻīlio nā iwi, a na ka pōpoki ka iʻa.
     7. Nāu nā pua pīkake i loko o ka pākini.
     8. Mahalo; e hoʻouna aku au (i nā pua) i ke kula na ke kumu.
     9. E mālama pono; ua hāʻawi aku kou makuahine i ke kālā nui no kēnā lole wāwae selamoku.
    10. ʻO ke kau hope loa kēia no Lia lāua ʻo Kawailani.
    11. Na lāua kēia mau makana.

E.   Ua loaʻa iaʻu ka haʻawina ʻōlelo Hawaiʻi i nehinei, akā, ʻaʻole maopopo iaʻu. Hiki paha iā Māpuana ke kōkua mai iaʻu. Maopopo iā ia ka ʻōlelo Hawaiʻi no ka mea, ʻōlelo Hawaiʻi kona mau mākua. ʻAʻole hiki iā Māpuana ke ʻōlelo Hawaiʻi, akā maopopo nō iā ia. I nehinei, ua loaʻa iā ia he leka ma ka ʻōlelo Hawaiʻi. Ua kākau ʻia e kona kupunahine. Ke noho nei ʻo ia ma Niʻihau. Maopopo ka ʻōlelo haole iā Tūtū, akā, makemake ʻo ia e kākau iā Māpuana ma ka ʻōlelo Hawaiʻi. Ua lawe mai ʻo Māpuana i kāna leka i ka papa i kēia lā. Ua hiki iā mākou apau ke heluhelu, akā, ua maopopo nā mea apau i loko o ka leka i ke kumu wale nō.

REVIEW 5

HO‘I HOPE ‘ELIMA

I. ANSWERS

A. 1. The old man was fed by the gods.
    2. The breadfruit will be picked by the farmer.
    3. That other tree was planted.
    4. My trousers were taken by my younger sibling.
    5. The clothes will be washed by me.
    6. Auē, e ho‘ouna ‘ia aku ana ku‘u ipo i ke kula ma Lāna‘i.
    7. Ua ho‘omaka ‘ia ka papa e Tuti.
    8. Ua ‘eli ‘ia ka imu e Keoki mā.
    9. Ua hānau ‘ia kā māua mo‘opuna mua loa i ka makahiki ‘umikūmāiwa kanahikukūmāiwa.
    10. Ua ho‘omo‘a ‘ia kēia mau ‘uala e ‘oe?

B. 1. Hiki ia‘u ke ho‘ouna aku i ke koena i ka hale noho haumana?
    2. Ua hiki i ke kumu lā‘au ‘ulu ke nalowale.
    3. ‘A‘ole i hiki iā mākou ke ho‘oma‘ama‘a i nehinei.
    4. Hiki ke loa‘a ka manakō ‘ono i Kona.
    5. Hiki ke kū‘ai ‘ia mai ka i‘a makamaka hou ma ka makeke ma ke ala nui Kekaulike.

C. 1. Maopopo iā ‘oukou ka ha‘awina hou?
    2. ‘A‘ole maopopo ia‘u kou kumu.
    3. ‘A‘ole i loa‘a kekahi kope o ka puke i ko‘u hoa lumi.
    4. E loa‘a ana ke ka‘a pipi‘i i kā mākou kumu i kēia kau a‘e.
    5. Ua loa‘a ka makana i ka ‘ohana apau.

D. 1. No'u kēnā pāpale lauhala.
2. Nou kēia lei 'awapuhi?
3. Na ke kumu kēia uku.
4. Ua kū'ai mai ka luna i ka mea'ono na nā kānaka apau.
5. Ua kū'ai mai mākou i ka pālule nona.

E. 1. Aloha nui loa 'o Mikela laua 'o Luhiehu kekahi i kekahi.
2. Ua waiho ka mahi'ai i kekahi mau hē'ī na ka 'ohana.
3. Inā 'oe makemake, hiki iā 'oe ke ho'omo'a i ka mai'a maka.
4. E 'olu'olu 'oe, e lawe mai i kekahi kope na ko'u hoa aloha.
5. I kekahi manawa, ua hiki mai ke akua 'o Kū i Hawai'i nei mai Kahiki mai.

19
HAʻAWINA ʻUMIKŪMĀIWA

I. TOPICS

A. *Lilo* as "taken, lost, relinquished"
B. *ʻAna* nominalizer
C. *ʻOle*

II. BASIC SENTENCE TARGETS

1. *Ua lilo* sentence
2. *Ua lilo* sentence with recipient
3. *Lilo loa* sentence with *ʻana*
4. *I . . . ʻana* (when) sentence with possessive pronoun and directional
5. *I . . . ʻana* (when) sentence with possessive noun
6. *I . . . ʻana* (when) sentence with direct object and directional; *lilo* with cause
7. Subject *ʻana* phrase with possessive pronoun
8. Subject *ʻana* phrase with possessive noun
9. *ʻAna* with passive and directional
10. *ʻAna* with *nō*
11. *ʻAna* with *ma hope; pākahi*
12. *ʻAna* with *ʻole*

III. DIALOGS

1. In the classroom

Hopoe: Kala, what's your problem?
Kala: Oh my goodness! My backpack is gone.
Hopoe: Was (it) left in this room?
Kala: Yes, I forgot it after class. When I came back, it was gone.
Hopoe: Maybe the teacher has it.
Kala: Maybe so. I'll call her.

2. On the telephone

Kala: Teacher, this is Kala. May I disturb you?
Pua: Hi, Kala. What do you want?
Kala: I forgot my backpack in the classroom, and it's gone.
Pua: Too bad! I don't have it. Is there a lot of money in the bag?
Kala: No, but my Hawaiian book is inside.
Pua: Tsā, that's a major problem. Give a big reward for the return of the book.
Kala: I can't, because I don't have the money.
Pua: Yeah, yeah. Don't cry; I understand. Maybe I can give you a new book.
Kala: Thanks, Pua; I'll give the payment to you after I graduate from the university.
Pua: No problem, Kala. It's my pleasure to help you.

3. At Lilinoe's restaurant

Lopaka: Did you hear the good news? Kimo's truck was returned yesterday.
Lilinoe: That truck was lost to a thief, wasn't it?
Lopaka: Yes, but the police caught the thief.
Lilinoe: Wow, lucky! How was the thief caught?
Lopaka: When he tried to sell the truck, he was caught by the cops.
Lilinoe: And how about the truck? Perhaps some things were missing?
Lopaka: No, no. The thief took good care of the truck.
Lilinoe: Is Kimo really happy at the truck being returned?
Lopaka: Yes, because they don't have any other car.

4. At Lilinoe's famous restaurant

Mahaʻoi: You there, may I bother you?
Lilinoe: Excuse me. I was totally involved in preparing this new dish.
Mahaʻoi: No big deal. I want my check, please.
Lilinoe: The bill is on the table.
Mahaʻoi: No. I looked, but didn't get it.
Lilinoe: Goodness! When the door was opened, maybe the wind got it.
Mahaʻoi: So maybe I don't have to pay you.
Lilinoe: No way! I haven't forgotten your order. I can write a new check.
Mahaʻoi: If I don't pay, what are the consequences?
Lilinoe: Tsā! I'll call the police, and you'll be taken by him.
Mahaʻoi: Don't you have a soft heart?

Lilinoe: No way; I'm calling the police.
Mahaʻoi: Don't do that. I'm only playing. Here's the check and my payment.
Lilinoe: Oh, you're a waste of time! Get out of here!

5. At the university

Pua: Tuti, look at my rascal class. They're totally absorbed in doing the exam.
Tuti: Yes, and after their writing, I'm going to question them one at a time.
Pua: Yes, they're very worried about that kind of performance.
Tuti: That's the consequences of not going to listen to the tapes.
Pua: Right. At the beginning of the semester, they go often, but later they don't go at all.
Tuti: It can't be helped. They have a lot of assignments in the other classes.
Pua: Tsā, Tuti! You have a soft heart.
Tuti: Because my attending the university isn't over, and I understand their problems.

IV. ANSWERS

A. "The Octopus and the Rat"

In the old days a rat lived with his family on the island of Mokoliʻi. (Nowadays, this place is called Chinaman's Hat.) One day he wanted to go to Kāneʻohe. He got a canoe and paddled to Kualoa. When he arrived, the canoe was fastened to a coconut tree, and the rat went to Kāneʻohe. But the canoe was not fastened properly. So when he arrived from Kāneʻohe, the canoe was lost at sea. Oh what a big problem! The rat sat down and cried with a very loud voice. His crying was heard by a good-hearted octopus. The octopus asked him, "Hey there, what's your problem?" And the rat answered, "My canoe has disappeared; maybe it went out to sea, because perhaps my mooring wasn't well done. I can't return to Mokoliʻi because I can't swim." The soft-hearted octopus replied, "No problem; maybe I can help you. Climb up on top of my head, and I'll take you back to your home." When the rat was settled on his head, the octopus began to return to Mokoliʻi. Oh how frightened the rat was, but the octopus called out, "Sit still! Don't be afraid! I am very familiar with this sea." After a while, they arrived at Mokoliʻi. The rat got down from on top of the octopus's head, and told him, "I am very grateful to you for your bringing me. There is a gift for you on top of your head," and the rat ran inland fast. The octopus felt on top of his head and got excrement. The rat had had a bowel movement on top of his head because he was so afraid. Oh, the octopus was so mad! From that time on, if a cowrie is seen by an octopus, he grabs it because he thinks it's the rat. The Pacific people make something called a "lūheʻe" with a rock and a cowrie, and they catch octopus with this device.

B. 1. I ka wā kahiko, ua noho kekahi ʻiole ma ka mokupuni ʻo Mokoli ʻi.
    2. I kekahi lā, ua hoe ʻo ia i Kualoa.
    3. Ua hoʻopaʻa ʻo ia i kona waʻa i ke kumu niu.
    4. Hele aku ʻo ia i Kāneʻohe.
    5. I kona hoʻi ʻana mai, ua lilo kona waʻa i ke kai.
    6. Noho ihola ka ʻiole a uē me ka leo nui.
    7. Ua lohe kekahi heʻe lokomaikaʻi i kona uē ʻana.
    8. Nīnau akula ʻo ia i ka ʻiole, "Eia nei, he aha kou pilikia?"
    9. Pane maila ka ʻiole, "Makemake au e hoʻi aku i ka hale.
    10. Akā, ʻaʻole hiki iaʻu ke ʻauʻau."
    11. Ua haʻi aku ka heʻe iā ia, " ʻAʻole pilikia.
    12. Hiki iaʻu ke kōkua aku iāʻoe.
    13. E piʻi aʻe ʻoe i luna o koʻu poʻo.
    14. E hoʻihoʻi aku au iā ʻoe."
    15. Ua makaʻu loa ka ʻiole.
    16. I ko lāua hiki ʻana i Mokoliʻi, ua lele ihola ka ʻiole.
    17. Haʻi akula ʻo ia, "Mahalo. Aia he makana nāu, ma luna o kou poʻo."
    18. A holo ʻāwīwī akula ʻo ia.
    19. Ua hāhā ka heʻe ma luna o kona poʻo.
    20. Loaʻa iā ia ke kūkae.
    21. I kēia manawa, inā ʻike ka heʻe i ka leho, lālau ʻo ia iā ia.
    22. Manaʻo ihola ʻo ia, ʻo ka heʻe ia.
    23. Hana ka poʻe Hawaiʻi i ka lūheʻe me ka leho a me ka pōhaku.
    24. Loaʻa ka heʻe iā lākou me kēia mea.

C. 1. kona hiki ʻana
    2. ka lālau ʻana o ka heʻe i ka lūheʻe
       ko ka heʻe lālau ʻana i ka lūheʻe
    3. he maiʻa maikaʻi no ke kuke ʻana
    4. i ka hāhā ʻana aʻe o ka heʻe i kona poʻo
       i ko ka heʻe hāhā ʻana aʻe i kona poʻo

     5. ma hope o ka lele ʻana iho o ka ʻiole
        ma hope o ko ka ʻiole lele ʻana iho
     6. ma mua o ke kapa ʻia ʻana o ka hale (passive)
        ma mua o ke kapa ʻana i ka hale (active)
     7. i ka hoʻomaka ʻana o ka papa
        i ko ka papa hoʻomaka ʻana
     8. ko Lilinoe hoʻomākaukau ʻana aku i ka lūʻau
        ka hoʻomākaukau ʻana aku o Lilinoe i ka lūʻau
     9. ko ke kumu heluhelu ʻana aʻe i ka moʻolelo
        ka heluhelu ʻana ʻae o ke kumu i ka moʻolelo
    10. koʻu ʻike ʻana aku i kaʻaihue

D. 1. He hana nui ka hoʻomākaukau ʻana i ka imu.
     2. I ka lālau ʻana aku o ka heʻe i ka lūheʻe, ua loaʻa ʻo ia i ka lawaiʻa.
       I ko ka heʻe lālau ʻana aku i ka lūheʻe, . . .
     3. Ma hope o ka lilo ʻana o kā ʻAuliʻi ʻeke, pīhoihoi loa ʻo ia.
     4. Ua lawe mai ʻo Kuʻupua i kāna koena no ka hānai ʻana aku i nā pōpoki wīwī loa.
     5. Ma mua o ka holoi ʻana i kona lole wāwae, ua hāhā kaʻu keiki kāne i loko o nā pākeke.
     6. Ua hauʻoli loa ʻo Pāpā i ka hana ʻana i ka lei hulu nona.
     7. ʻAʻole i makemake ʻo Akaka i ka hoʻohenehene ʻana o nā kaikamāhine iā ia.
       . . . i ko nā kaikamāhine hoʻohenehene ʻana iā ia.
     8. Hoʻomaʻamaʻa pū kā Pua mau haumana ma mua o ko lākou hoʻomaka ʻana i ka hōʻike.
     9. He hana nanea ke kākau ʻana aʻe i ka leka i kuʻu ipo.
    10. E kiʻi aku ʻoe i ka hēʻī maka naʻu no ka hoʻoluʻolu ʻana i kēia mau nahu ʻuku.

E. 1. Ua lilo ʻo Bathsheba iā Kawika.
     2. E lilo ana ʻoe iaʻu.
     3. Ua lilo loa ʻo Lene mā i ka nānā ʻana i ke kiʻiʻoniʻoni.
     4. Ua lilo paha kāu kālā i ka holoi ʻana o kou māmā i kou pālule.
       . . . i ko kou māmā holoi ʻana i kou pālule.
     5. Ua lilo pākahi nā iʻa liʻiliʻi i ka manō pōloli.
     6. Auē, lilo ke kaikamahine uʻi loa i ka ʻelemakule waiwai.
     7. Ua lilo ka ʻiole momona i ka pōpoki, akā, ma hope iho, ua lilo ka pōpoki i ka ʻīlio hana ʻino.
     8. Ua lilo kona ola i kona luʻu ʻana iho ma waena o nā pōhaku.
     9. Ua lilo nā keiki i ko lāua mau mākua hānai.
    10. E lilo ana ka ʻāina o ke kamaʻāina i ke Kepanī.

20

HAʻAWINA IWAKĀLUA

I. TOPICS

A. Actor-emphatic sentence
B. *Lilo* as "become (turn into a X)"

II. BASIC SENTENCE TARGETS

1. Completed action actor-emphatic sentence; *na wai*
2. Completed action actor-emphatic sentence; *na* X
3. *E* verb actor-emphatic sentence; *nāna*
4. *E* verb actor-emphatic sentence; *naʻu*
5. *E* verb actor-emphatic sentence; *na* + noun phrase
6. *Lilo* (become) sentence
7. *Lilo* (become) sentence with *ʻana*

III. DIALOGS

1. At Lilinoe's restaurant

Mahaʻoi: Lilinoe, who prepared this dried fish?
Lilinoe: It was Lopaka who dried it. Why? Isn't it tasty?
Mahaʻoi: No; it's very delicious. Does he make all the Hawaiian food for the restaurant?
Lilinoe: No; I cook most of the food. Lopaka only does the raw food.
Mahaʻoi: Isn't he working at the police station?
Lilinoe: Yes, he's working there. But on the nonworking days, he helps me here.
Mahaʻoi: Where is he today?

Lilinoe: He and Koleka went to Honomū.
Maha'oi: Why? To see Akaka Falls?
Lilinoe: No. Koleka's father is living there. They are visiting her
            father.

2. At Koleka's house in Honomū

Koleka: Papa, have you heard? Kalekona wants to become a musi-
           cian.
Papa: Tsā, this grandchild is a waste of time. It might be better if he
           becomes a policeman like his father.
Koleka: But he doesn't like that kind of work.
Papa: How about a lawyer? There's a lot of money if he becomes a
           lawyer.
Koleka: He is very excited about playing music. Money is not an
           important thing.
Papa: Wow, he's lucky. The two of you give him money?
Koleka: No. He's working at Lilinoe's restaurant during the day. In
           the evening he plays music at various places.
Papa: And what? Does he sing too?
Koleka: No; he's kind of shy. So he plays music and his friends sing.

3. At the university

Kawailani: Pua, when you graduated from the university, did you
            become a Hawaiian language teacher?
Pua: No; I became an English teacher for students from foreign
            countries.
Kawailani: Was that interesting work?
Pua: In the beginning, it was kind of interesting, but later I
            didn't like it.
Kawailani: Weren't the students good?
Pua: Yes, the majority of them only wanted to play.
Kawailani: Not like us! We are excited about studying the Hawaiian
            language assignments.
Pua: Tsā! Get out of here!

4. On Kaho'olawe

Alaka'i: Tsā, who dried this towel close to the fire?
Keoni: I did that. What's the problem?
Alaka'i: The towel stinks for smoke. Dry the towel in the sun.
Keoni: Like those octopuses over there?

Alakaʻi: Yes, like that. Whose octopuses are those?

Keoni: We got the octopus using the lūheʻe. We crave dried octopus.

Alakaʻi: Me too. After drying, broil the octopus over the fire.

Keoni: And eat it with poi! Oh that's so delicious with beer.

Alakaʻi: Have you eaten raw octopus? That was a common food when I was a kid.

Keoni: I haven't eaten that kind of octopus. What's the preparation?

Alakaʻi: My tūtū would massage the raw octopus with salt until it was soft, and then I would eat it.

Keoni: You didn't learn the preparation?

Alakaʻi: No. I was very stupid when I was a kid. I didn't learn the everyday activities of my grandparents.

Keoni: What a waste. That style of living is totally lost.

5. On the telephone at the dorm

Leilehua: Mealani, Uncle ʻIokepa is picking you up. We're going to the restaurant.

Mealani: Thanks, Aunty, but I can't! When I became a student, my work ended. I don't have any money nowadays.

Leilehua: Tsā, Mealani! You're a stupid girl! I'll pay. That's the usual role of aunties.

Mealani: Yes, I know. But I am very embarrassed. You folks always pay for me.

Leilehua: Not at all. And you often help me too with watching the kids.

Mealani: It's my pleasure to watch them. You guys are my family.

Leilehua: Yes, that's right, so we'll pay. After you become a Hawaiian language teacher, you can take us to a really expensive restaurant.

Mealani: Oh, I hear Uncle calling me.

Leilehua: Good. You guys come quickly! Bye.

IV. ANSWERS

A. "About Akaka Falls"

In the old days, a boy named Akaka lived with his grandmother in Honomū on the island of Hawaiʻi. Akaka always played with two girls every day. One evening, his grandmother washed his loincloth and dried the loincloth over the fire. The next morning, Akaka put on his loincloth and went outside to play with the girls. For goodness sake! They teased him a lot because his loincloth smelled of smoke. Too bad! He was so embarrassed, and he ran quickly home and cried to his grandmother. After that, he climbed with his dog above the waterfall close to his house, and they jumped down. They died and turned into rocks right under the waterfall. The boy is a big rock, and the dog is a little rock. His grandmother was very sad, and she turned into a big rock too, above the waterfall. These three rocks are there until today. That waterfall is called "Akaka" even now.

C. 1. E lilo ana ka 'elemakule i kupuna ma ke kula 'o Noelani.
2. I kona hele 'ana aku i ke kula nui, ua lilo 'o Mikioi i kuene.
3. Ua lilo ko Akaka kupunahine i pōhaku nui ma luna a'e o ka wailele.
4. Ua lilo kā Akaka 'īlio i pōhaku li'ili'i ma lalo iho o ka wailele.

D. 1. Na ka he'e i ho'iho'i aku i ka 'iole i Mokoli'i.
2. Ua 'ōlelo aku ka he'e, "Na'u e kōkua aku iā 'oe."
3. Na ke kaikamahine hana nui i pūlehu i ka 'uala.
4. E hele kākou i ke ki'i'oni'oni; na Hopoe e uku.

E. 1. How old are you?
2. What's the name of your parents?
3. How many children are there in your family?
4. How many girls are there in your family?
5. How many boys are there in your family?
6. Do you have a dog?
7. Do you have a bird?
8. Who prepared your breakfast?
9. After graduation, what will you become?
10. Did Akaka have a cat?

F. 1. Na wai i hānai i kou kaikua'ana?
2. Na ko'u mau kūpuna i hānai iā ia.
3. Na wai i hānai iā 'oe?
4. Na ko'u kaikua'ana i hānai ia'u.
5. Na wai e hānai i kāu mau keiki?
6. Na'u e hānai iā lākou.
7. Na wai e kaula'i nei i ka i'a?
8. Na Kini e kaula'i nei i ka i'a.
9. Na wai e hana (or ho'omākaukau) i ka laiki?
10. Nāna (e hana).
11. Na'u e ha'i aku iā ia.

21

HAʻAWINA IWAKĀLUAKŪMĀKAHI

I. TOPICS

A. Situation-emphatic sentences
B. "When" expressions
C. Telling time
D. Time phrases

II. BASIC SENTENCE TARGETS

1. Situation-emphatic sentence with pronoun subject; *ināhea . . . i* verb *ai*
2. Situation-emphatic sentence with noun subject; *āhea e* verb *ai*
3. Situation-emphatic sentence with noun subject; *i ka hola ʻehia*
4. Situation-emphatic sentence with pronoun subject; *e* verb *nei; no ke aha*
5. Situation-emphatic sentence with pronoun subject; *pehea*
6. Situation-emphatic sentence with pronoun subject; *i hea*
7. Situation-emphatic sentence with pronoun subject; *aia i hea*
8. Situation-emphatic sentence with pronoun subject; *hapahā hola* X
9. Situation-emphatic sentence with pronoun subject; *hapalua hola* X
10. Situation-emphatic sentence with pronoun subject; *ma* X (place)
11. *Ke* (whenever)
12. *Kokoke* (preceding stative verb)

III. DIALOGS

1. At the university

ʻAlena: Hepualei, when did you arrive at the university today?
Hepualei: Six oʻclock is when I arrived.
ʻAlena: Goodness, why did you come in the early morning?
Hepualei: I like to park the car close to the university.
ʻAlena: When will you return home?
Hepualei: Whenever my classes are finished, I'll go back. Maybe at three or four oʻclock.
ʻAlena: Aren't you tired?
Hepualei: No, because I go to sleep at eight thirty.

2. In the Hawaiian language class

Wili: Laiana, when will this class end?
Laiana: Twenty minutes after eleven.
Wili: Wow, how long! I'm not interested in this lesson.
Laiana: Me too! Where will you go after class?
Wili: Maybe to the cafeteria. Let's go drink beer!
Laiana: I can't; I start work at one oʻclock.
Wili: Where are you working now?
Laiana: I'm working at the university.
Wili: Tsā, that's not a problem. You can go with me to Mānoa Gardens. There's a lot of time.
Laiana: Maybe can. What time is it?
Wili: Quarter past eleven. This class is almost finished.

3. At the university

Kani: Pua, how do you come to town?
Pua: Most of the time I come with my friend. But some days, it's my husband who brings me.
Kani: You have a good-hearted husband! He doesn't work here in Honolulu, does he?
Pua: Kahaluʻu is where he is working, but now and then he has work in town.
Kani: I don't understand; what is his job?
Pua: He's a minister at St. John's By The Sea Church.
Kani: And you are the minister's wife? *(He laughs.)*
Pua: Hey, why are you laughing?

Kani: Excuse me. You are an unusual minister's wife.

Pua: Not at all. If you come to my church, you can watch me in that kind of role.

4. On the telephone at Lilinoe's restaurant

Mahaʻoi: Good morning. What time will the restaurant open?

Kalekona: Quarter to six is when I opened the door.

Mahaʻoi: Wow, so early in the morning! Is Lilinoe there?

Kalekona: No; at eight thirty she may come in.

Mahaʻoi: I have a question. Day before yesterday, I ate some really delicious Portuguese pork. Do you have it today?

Kalekona: Not today. I'm the one who makes that kind of pork. Day after tomorrow that item will be available.

Mahaʻoi: Why won't it be available today?

Kalekona: Because I soak the pork in vinegar for three days, and after that I cook it.

Mahaʻoi: Please reserve a table for my wife and me on that day.

Kalekona: Okay. Thanks for calling.

IV. ANSWERS

A.   1. Ināhea ʻoe i hānau ʻia ai?
      2. Ināhea i hānau ʻia ai kou mau mākua?
      3. Ma hea ʻoe i hānau ʻia ai?
      4. Ma hea i hānau ʻia ai kou mau mākua?
      5. Aia i hea ʻoe e noho nei?
      6. Aia i hea e noho nei kou mau mākua?
      7. I ka hola ʻehia ʻoe i hele mai ai i ke kula i kēia kakahiaka?
      8. Pehea ʻoe i hele mai ai i ke kula?
      9. I ka hola ʻehia ʻoe e hoʻi aku ai i ka hale?
     10. Pehea ʻoe e hoʻi aku ai i ka hale?
     11. No ke aha ʻoe i hele mai ai i ke kula nui o Hawaiʻi?
     12. Aia i hea ʻoe e hana nei?
     13. Āhea e pau ai ke kau?
     14. I hea ʻoe e hele ai i kēia kau wela?
     15. No ke aha ʻoe i aʻo ʻole ai i ka ʻōlelo Kepanī?
     16. Ma hea ʻoe i kūʻai ai i kou kāmaʻa?
     17. Ma hea ʻoe e ʻai ai i ka ʻaina awakea i kēia lā?
     18. No ke aha ʻoe e aʻo nei i ka ʻōlelo Hawaiʻi?
     19. Āhea ʻoe e puka ai?
     20. I ka lā hea ʻoe e hele ʻole mai ai i ka papa?

B.   1. kēlā makahiki aku nei
      2. kēia pule aʻe
      3. kēlā makahiki aku nei a ia makahiki aku
      4. kēia pule aʻe a ia pule aku
      5. i nehinei a ia lā aku
      6. (ka lā) ʻapōpō a ia lā aku
      7. kēlā mahina aku nei
      8. hola ʻekahi
      9. hapalua hola ʻumikūmālua
     10. hapahā hola ʻumi
     11. hapahā i hala ka hola ʻeono
     12. iwakālua minuke ma mua o ka hola ʻelima
     13. ʻumi minuke i hala ka hola ʻekolu
         ʻumi minuke ma hope o ka hola ʻekolu

REVIEW 6
HOʻI HOPE ʻEONO

I. ANSWERS

A.   1. E lilo ana ʻo ia i kahuna pule ma hope o kona puka ʻana.
      2. Ua lilo ʻo Nāhoa i lōio i kēlā makahiki aku nei.
      3. E lilo ana ʻo Kawehi i makuahine i kēia kau aʻe.
      4. Ua lilo ko ka ʻiole waʻa.
      5. Ua lilo ke kālā a ka wahine naʻau palupalu i ka ʻaihue.

B.   1. Ma hope o ke kaulaʻi ʻana o koʻu kaikunāne i ke aku, kūʻai aku ʻo ia i ko Lilinoe hale ʻaina.
        Ma hope o ko koʻu kaikunāne kaulaʻi ʻana i ke aku, . . .
      2. I ka lilo ʻana o nā hoe i ke kai, ʻaʻole i hiki iā lākou ke hoʻihoʻi i ka waʻa.
      3. ʻO ia ka hopena o ka inu ʻana i ka pia ma mua o ka hoe waʻa.
      4. I ka hāhā ʻana o ka ʻiole ma luna o kona poʻo, ua hoka loa ʻo ia.
        I ko ka ʻiole hāhā ʻana ma luna o kona poʻo, . . .
      5. Ma mua o ke kāhea ʻana i ka mele, e hoʻomaʻamaʻa i nā huaʻōlelo Hawaiʻi!

C.   1. Na ka heʻe e lālau i ka leho.
      2. Na ka ʻiole i kiʻo ma luna o ko ka heʻe poʻo.
      3. Na ke kumu kolohe i haʻi mai i kēia moʻolelo iā mākou.
      4. Nāna e kākau i nā haʻawina ʻano ʻē.
      5. Naʻu i kapa i ka inoa Hawaiʻi no ka wahine a kaʻu keiki kāne.

D.   1. Ināhea i loaʻa ai ka hopena iā ʻoe?
      2. Āhea e loaʻa ai ka naʻaukake Pukikī?
      3. I ka lā ʻapōpō a ia lā aku e mākaukau ai.
      4. Ma hea ʻoe i hoʻokuʻu ai i ke kaʻa?
      5. Ma waena o ke ala nui hele ʻole ʻia au i waiho ai i kou kalaka.

22

HAʻAWINA IWAKĀLUAKŪMĀLUA

I. TOPICS

A. Possessive locational sentences
B. *Ia* (aforementioned)
C. *Like; e like me*
D. Colors

II. BASIC SENTENCE TARGETS

1. Possessive locational sentence with noun location
2. Possessive locational sentence with pronoun location
3. Possessive locational sentence with *eia*
4. Possessive locational sentence; *ia* (aforementioned)
5. *Ia* (aforementioned) as object
6. *Ia* (aforementioned) with *ma*
7. *Ia* (aforementioned) following passive *ʻia*
8. *Like* (as main verb)
9. *Like . . . me*
10. *E like me*

III. DIALOGS

1. At Luika's house

Makia: Mama, where are my jeans?
Luika: Your older sister has your new pants.
Makia: Why? Doesn't she have pants?
Luika: She didn't wash clothes.

Makia: Oh how lazy! When did she take these pants?
Luika: This morning is when she put them on. Didn't she ask you?
Makia: No way! And my friend has my other pants. I can't go to school.
Luika: Tsā! Put on a muʻumuʻu and go!
Makia: No. The other girls will tease me.
Luika: Don't argue with me, Makia! Put on your clothes and go to school.
Makia: But how will I go? The bus has already gone.
Luika: Walk right now! It's almost eight o'clock.

2. Before Hawaiian language class

Pua: Kuʻupua, where is your Hawaiian language book?
Kuʻupua: My mother has that book.
Pua: Why did you give your book to her?
Kuʻupua: She wants to learn Hawaiian, but she can't go to school.
Pua: And how are you going to study the new assignment?
Kuʻupua: When class is over, I'll go to buy another book.
Pua: It's not possible to buy this book in the bookstore. I'm the only one who makes copies.
Kuʻupua: Oh, I didn't know. Perhaps you could make a copy for me?
Pua: Yes, okay. And today, sit close to Kiaka and look at his book.
Kuʻupua: Thank you teacher. I'll give you the money for the book.

3. In ʻEkekela's office

Kunāne: ʻEkekela, where's your car today?
ʻEkekela: ʻAlapaki has my car. He couldn't start his truck this morning.
Kunāne: How did you come to work?
ʻEkekela: It was ʻAlapaki who brought me.
Kunāne: What's the trouble with the truck?
ʻEkekela: I don't understand that kind of thing. His friend is the one who will fix it.
Kunāne: Is that his profession?
ʻEkekela: Yes, he's coming to the house after work to look at everything.
Kunāne: When are you going back home?
ʻEkekela: Quarter past five maybe. When his work is finished, ʻAlapaki is picking me up.

Kunāne: If you want to go before that, I can take you back at four thirty.

ʻEkekela: That's good. I can prepare the pūpū for ʻAlapaki "guys."

4. At Lilinoe's restaurant

Lopaka: Lilinoe, have you seen the new restaurant?

Lilinoe: No. Where is this restaurant?

Lopaka: It's on Waiānuenue Avenue, close to the post office.

Lilinoe: What's the kind of food at this place?

Lopaka: I don't really know, because I haven't gone inside. But this restaurant is called The Portuguese Sausage.

Lilinoe: Call Koleka and let's go eat lunch there together.

Lopaka: Up to you, but who will work here?

Lilinoe: Kalekona will cook lunch. He knows the preparation of everything.

Lopaka: When will he arrive?

Lilinoe: Quarter to ten. We can go at half past eleven.

Lopaka: I'll pick Koleka up, because Kalekona has her car.

Lilinoe: Why? Where is his Jeep?

Lopaka: It died last week. That car is an old thing.

5. In Kawehi's office

Tuti: Kawehi, my keys are lost.

Kawehi: No. I have your keys.

Tuti: How did you get these keys?

Kawehi: When you came to my office this morning, you left the keys on top of my desk.

Tuti: Oh I'm so happy! There's so much trouble if keys are lost.

Kawehi: Yeah, right. Can't drive the car, can't get inside of the house.

Tuti: Yes, I was really worried. I searched in my purse, in the office, in the classroom, in the road, but didn't get them.

Kawehi: Excuse me. I thought you knew the keys were here.

Tuti: No problem. Getting them is the main thing. Let's go eat lunch. I'll treat.

Kawehi: I have classes until twelve thirty.

Tuti: It's nothing. We can go at one o'clock.

Kawehi: Thanks, Tuti. Bye.

6. At Luika's house

Makia: Mama, I want new shoes like Laʻe's shoes.
Luika: Why? Your shoes are the same.
Makia: No way! She has pink shoes. I've got orange shoes. Pink and orange aren't the same.
Luika: That's not important. New shoes are really expensive.
Makia: But I can't wear orange shoes with my new purple dress.
Luika: Ask Laʻe to lend you her shoes.
Makia: Tsā! The size of her feet isn't the same as mine. I have very small feet.
Luika: You are a conceited girl!
Makia: Please, Mama, I can buy the shoes with my own money.
Luika: It's up to you, but it's a waste of money.

IV. ANSWERS

A. 1. Aia iā wai ko ʻAuliʻi ʻeke kua?
   Aia ko ʻAuliʻi ʻeke kua iā wai?
   2. Aia ia ʻeke kua i ke kumu.
   3. Aia iā ʻoe ka helu kelepona a ka lōio?
   Aia ka helu kelepona a ka lōio iā ʻoe?
   4. Eia iaʻu kona inoa.
   Eia kona inoa iaʻu.
   5. Aia ko ʻAlapaki kaʻa iā Kimo.

B. 1. Aia ia keʻena i ka hale ʻo Spalding.
   2. ʻOno loa au i ia ʻano heʻe.
   3. Ua loaʻa ka heʻe i ia mea.
   4. Na ia kahuna pule i hīmeni i ka Lāpule.
   5. ʻAno ʻē ia māmā kahu.

C. 1. E holoholo ana ʻo ia e like me ke kanaka pūpule.
   2. Ua like kou ihu me ka maiʻa.
   3. Ua like loa nā hoahānau.
   4. ʻAʻole hana ʻo Pua e like me nā māmā kahu ʻē aʻe.
   5. ʻAʻole ʻono ka pūpū haole e like me ka pūpū Hawaiʻi.

D. " ʻO Kāne lāua ʻo Kū"

I ka wā kahiko, ua noho kekahi ʻelemakule i Hilo. Hoihoi loa ʻo ia i ka pule ʻana. Ua pule ʻo ia iā Kāne lāua ʻo Kū i kēlā me kēia manawa. Ma mua o ka ʻai ʻana, pule ʻo ia. Ke ʻo ia hele i ka mahi'ai, pule mua 'o ia. Ke ho'i 'o ia i ka hiamoe, pule hou nō 'o ia. Ua pule ia 'elemakule i ka lā apau.

I kekahi manawa, ua hele akula ia 'elemakule i ka lawai'a me kekahi mau hoa aloha. Ua lu'u ihola 'o ia i lalo o ke kai. Kali kona mau hoa aloha i luna a'e, akā, 'a'ole 'o ia i puka a'e. Mana'o lākou, ua make 'o ia, a ho'i lākou i ka hale.

Akā, 'a'ole i make ia 'elemakule. I kona lu'u 'ana, ua 'ike 'o ia i ka 'āina nani ma lalo o ke kai. Aia kekahi hale me nā māla pua. I ka hele 'ana o ka 'elemakule kokoke i ka hale, ua lohe 'o ia i 'elua mau leo e kāhea ana iā ia. Komo 'o ia i loko o ka hale a 'ike i 'elua mau kāne e noho ana. Ua kono lāua iā ia e 'ai i ka 'aina ahiahi. Ma hope o ko lākou 'ai 'ana, ua ho'i akula ka 'elemakule i ka hiamoe no ka mea, māluhiluhi 'o ia.

I ke kakahiaka a'e ma hope o ka 'aina kakahiaka, ha'i mai nā kāne 'elua iā ia, " 'O māua 'o Kāne a me Kū. Lohe mau māua i kou kāhea pinepine 'ana mai iā māua. 'Ano hau'oli māua i kou kāhea 'ole 'ana mai ke 'oe hele i ka lua. Akā, he mea ho'onāukiuki iā māua kou pule mau 'ana. Eia ka hana pono: ke 'oe 'ala, e pule mai iā māua. Inā he pilikia kou, pule hou. Ke ho'i aku 'oe i ka hiamoe, e pule mai. Akā, i ka hapanui o ka manawa, mai kāhea mai iā māua. Inā māua makemake iā 'oe, e kāhea a'e māua iā 'oe. Hiki iā 'oe ke ho'i aku i kou hale i kēia manawa."

Ua ho'i akula ka 'elemakule i Hilo a noho ihola 'o ia i laila a hiki i kona make 'ana. Akā, ua pau kona pule 'ana i ka manawa apau.

23

HA'AWINA IWAKĀLUAKŪMĀKOLU

I. TOPICS

A. Type-A relative clauses
B. Negative class-inclusion and equational sentences
C. *Pono*

II. BASIC SENTENCE TARGETS

1. Type-A relative clause (*i* verb)
2. Type-A relative clause *(e* verb *nei)*
3. Type-A relative clause *(e* verb *ana)*
4. Type-A relative clause *(i* verb *'ia)*
5. Type-A relative clause *(e* verb *nei)*
6. Type-A relative clause *(e* verb)
7. Negative equational sentence
8. Negative class-inclusion sentence
9. *Pono* sentence with *e* verb
10. *Pono* sentence with *e* verb (no subject)

III. DIALOGS

1. At the dorm

'Auli'i: I'm really angry at the person who stole my backpack.
Mikioi: Maybe it wasn't stolen, 'Auli'i. You should go to the "lost and found" office.
'Auli'i: Where is this office?

Mikioi: I don't really know, but I know a woman who works there.
'Auli'i: Maybe you could ask her.
Mikioi: Okay. When I know, I'll call you.

2. At the "lost and found" office

Kahumea: Hello. Are you the student who is looking for the back-pack?
'Auli'i: Yes, did Mikioi tell you?
Kahumea: Yes. A lot of backpacks have been returned. What kind of backpack is yours?
'Auli'i: It's a black bag. My name wasn't written inside.
Kahumea: Tsā, that's stupid. You should write your name on your things. Perhaps this is your bag?
'Auli'i: That's not my bag. That's an old bag, and it's ugly too. My bag is a good one and very expensive too.
Kahumea: If that's the case, it was probably taken by a thief.
'Aulu'i: Oh, wow! It's the bag that was given to me by my grand-mother. She's going to be mad at me.
Kahumea: It can't be helped. How about it, maybe you can buy an identical bag, and she won't know.
'Auli'i: Tsā! That's not a proper thing to do! And besides, I don't have enough money.

3. At Lilinoe's restaurant

Lilinoe: Kalekona, this isn't a fish that was dried by your father.
Kalekona: Yes, Uncle Kimo sent this fish from Kona.
Lilinoe: Why? I have to explain to the people who buy it.
Kalekona: There was a lot of rain last week. There wasn't a sunny day for the drying.
Lilinoe: This kind of fish isn't good. Lopaka's fish is the most delicious.
Kalekona: Maybe so, but it is said by the grandfolks, "Eat what is available."
Lilinoe: That's not a good saying for a restaurant. If I talk like that to the people who come, goodness, they'll quickly go somewhere else.
Kalekona: Yeah, you have to speak very politely in a restaurant.

4. At Lilinoe's restaurant

Maha'oi: Lilinoe, who is that new person who is cooking?
Lilinoe: That's my nephew. His name is Kalekona.
Maha'oi: Who are his parents?
Lilinoe: Lopaka and Koleka. They only have one child.
Maha'oi: This Portuguese pork that was cooked by him is really delicious. Was it his mother who taught him?
Lilinoe: I don't know. You ought to ask him.
Maha'oi: I don't want to be nosy to him.
Lilinoe: That's not a nosy question. He will be very happy at your appreciating his work.

IV. ANSWERS

A. 1. ke keiki kāne hanauna i ho'oluhi i kona 'anakē
    2. ke kahuna pule i aloha nui 'ia
    3. ka lōio e kū'ai mai ana i ke ka'a pipi'i
    4. ke kumu e wehewehe ana i ka ha'awina
    5. ke 'eke kua i 'aihue 'ia
    6. ka mo'olelo e 'ōlelo 'ia mai ana iā mākou
    7. ke kanaka e ho'oku'u ana i ke ka'a
    8. ka mea ho'okani pila i hīmeni
    9. ka po'e e mālama i ka 'āina
   10. nā mea 'ai e kuke 'ia e Kalekona

B. 1. Ua 'ike au i ke kanaka i 'aihue i ke 'eke kua.
    2. 'O Akaka ka inoa o ke keiki kāne i lele iho mai luna iho o ka wailele.
    3. Ua loha 'oe i ka mo'olelo e pili ana i ka wahine i hānau i ke keiki manō?
    4. Ua māluhiluhi nō nā kānaka (ka po'e) i hiki mai i ke kakahiaka nui.
    5. 'A'ole maika'i ka makana i waiho 'ia e ka 'iole.
    6. E hā'awi aku i kēia mea 'ono i nā haumana e kōkua nei i ke kumu.
    7. Ke kali nei mākou i ka wahine e ho'iho'i mai ana i kā mākou hō'ike.
    8. E ho'omākaukau ana 'o Kalekona i ka 'aina awakea na nā kānaka e hele mai ana.
    9. Aia iā 'oe ka ha'awina e wehewehe 'ia ana i ka lā 'apōpō?

C. 1. 'A'ole 'o ia he keiki kāne nīele.
   2. 'A'ole kēnā he pālule pupuka loa.
   3. 'A'ole 'o Lilinoe he wahine na'au palupalu.
   4. 'A'ole 'o nehinei he lā mālie.
   5. 'A'ole ka māmā kahu he wahine 'ano 'ē.
   6. 'A'ole 'o Lilinoe ko Kalekona 'anakē.
   7. 'A'ole ka'u keiki kāne hanauna ka mea ho'okani pila.
   8. 'A'ole kāu kumu ko'u māmā. or 'A'ole ko'u māmā kāu kumu.
   9. 'A'ole kēia pūpū ka mea 'ai ono loa ma 'ane'i.
  10. 'A'ole 'o ia ke keiki ho'okano loa i kēia 'ohana.

   1. He's not the nosy boy.
   2. That's not a very ugly shirt.
   3. Lilinoe is not a soft-hearted woman.
   4. Yesterday wasn't a calm day.
   5. The minister's wife isn't a strange woman.
   6. Lilinoe isn't Kalekona's aunt.
   7. The musician isn't my nephew. or vice versa
   8. My mother isn't your teacher. or vice versa
   9. This pūpū isn't the most delicious food here.
  10. He's not the most conceited child in this family.

D. 1. 'A'ole ko'u kaikua'ana he wahine moloā.
   2. 'A'ole kēia he pūpū 'ono loa.
   3. 'A'ole au he kanaka nīele.
   4. 'A'ole lākou he mau haumana.
   5. 'A'ole 'o Lopaka he māka'i i kēia manawa.
   6. 'A'ole ka lā 'apōpō ka Lāpule.
   7. 'A'ole 'o 'Auli'i ka'u mo'opuna.
   8. 'A'ole kēlā luahine ka 'aihue.
   9. 'A'ole kēlā 'elemakule ke kumu 'ōlelo Pākē.
  10. 'A'ole 'o Luika ka muli loa i ko'u 'ohana.

E. 1. Pono 'oukou e kōkua kekahi i kekahi.
   2. Pono nā mākua e wehewehe i nā 'ōpiopio.
   3. Pono kākou e ho'omaka i ka papa.
   4. Pono 'o 'Alapaki e kū'ai mai i ke kalaka hou.

24

HAʻAWINA IWAKĀLUAKŪMĀHĀ

I. TOPICS

A. Type-B relative clauses

II. BASIC SENTENCE TARGETS

All the target sentences are variations of Type-B relative clauses; the list below describes the kind of Type-B clause.

1. Completed action, possessive proper noun subject
2. Completed action, possessive pronoun subject *(āna)*
3. Completed action, possessive pronoun subject *(aʻu)*
4. Completed action, possessive pronoun subject
5. Present tense, fronted possessive pronoun subject *(kā kākou)*
6. Completed action, fronted possessive pronoun subject *(kaʻu)*
7. Completed action, possessive pronoun subject *(aʻu)*
8. Completed action, o-possessive (reason)
9. Incomplete action, o-possessive (time)
10. Achieved state, noun subject (inanimate)
11. Achieved state, noun subject (inanimate)

III. DIALOGS

1. At Lilinoe's restaurant

ʻAlapaki: Have you seen the book that Pua wrote?
Lilinoe: Yes, a copy was brought by Kalekona.
ʻAlapaki: How did he get the book?

Lilinoe: He bought the book when he went to Honolulu.
ʻAlapaki: Do you know the store where the book was bought?
Lilinoe: No, but it doesn't matter. You can't read this book.
ʻAlapaki: Hey, don't put me down. I can read!
Lilinoe: This book is written in Hawaiian. I only understand our names.
ʻAlapaki: What? Are we in the book?
Lilinoe: Yes, she wrote about the things we do.
ʻAlapaki: Oh my goodness! We ought to learn Hawaiian.

2. At Lilinoe's restaurant

Mahaʻoi: I heard Kalekona is moving to Honolulu.
Lilinoe: Yes, he went yesterday.
Mahaʻoi: What's the reason he moved?
Lilinoe: He will become a student at the university.
Mahaʻoi: What a pity! The Portuguese food he cooked was so delicious.
Lilinoe: After he graduates, he's coming back.
Mahaʻoi: When will he graduate?
Lilinoe: I don't really know when he will graduate. Maybe a few years more.
Mahaʻoi: I can't wait! Maybe there's another restaurant that has this kind of food?
Lilinoe: Maybe The Portuguese Sausage has. Go there.

3. At the dorm

Kenike: ʻAulani, I want to see your new shoes.
ʻAulani: Here is what I bought. And here is something small for you.
Kenike: Thanks a lot, ʻAulani. Why did you give this present for me?
ʻAulani: Because you always help me with my homework.
Kenike: It's nothing. It's the stuff I learned last semester.
ʻAulani: Open the thing I gave you.
Kenike: The tape of Hawaiian music sung by Haunani Apoliona! I'm so happy!
ʻAulani: Have you heard this tape already?
Kenike: No, but I heard her at the lūʻau last weekend. The songs that she composed are so beautiful.

IV. ANSWERS

A. 1. the sweet potato that the girl is broiling
   2. the trousers that Lilinoe sent
   3. the rat that the octopus helped
   4. the assignment that the teacher will explain
   5. the gift that the rat gave to the octopus
   6. the loincloth that the grandmother dried
   7. the house where I live
   8. the day that my dog died
   9. the hour when the plane will arrive
   10. the place where the yellow ginger grows

B. 1. ka puke a Pua i kākau ai
      kā Pua puke i kākau ai
   2. ke kumu o kaʻu keiki kāne hanauna e neʻe ai i Honolulu
      ko kaʻu keiki kāne hanauna kumu e neʻe ai i Honolulu
      ke kumu i neʻe ai koʻu keiki kāne hanauna i Honolulu
   3. ke kaikamahine a ka mākaʻi e kōkua nei
      kā ka mākaʻi kaikamahine e kōkua nei
      ke kaikamahine e kokua nei ka mākaʻi
   4. ke kaona oʻu i hānau ʻia ai
      koʻu kaona i hānau ʻia ai
   5. ke ala nui i make ai ko Hepualei kaʻa
   6. ke kau o Kalani e puka ai
      ko Kalani kau e puka ai
      ke kau e puka ai ʻo Kalani
   7. ka ʻaina awakea a Lilinoe i kuke ai
      kā Lilinoe ʻaina awakea i kuke ai
      ka ʻaina awakea i kuke ai ʻo Lilinoe
   8. ke wailele o Akaka i lele iho ai
      ko Akaka wailele i lele iho ai
      ka wailele i lele iho ai ʻo Akaka
   9. ke kumu lāʻau o ke kaikamahine i piʻi aʻe ai
      ko ke kaikamahine kumu lāʻau i piʻi aʻe ai
      ke kumu lāʻau i piʻi aʻe ai ke kaikamahine
   10. ka hale kūʻai i loaʻa ai ka iʻa maloʻo ʻono
   11. ke lole hou āna e komo nei
       kāna lole hou e komo nei
   12. ka moʻolelo a ke kahuna pule e haʻi aku ai
       kā ke kahuna pule moʻolelo e haʻi aku ai
       ka moʻolelo e haʻi aku ai ke kahuna pule

REVIEW 7
HO'I HOPE 'EHIKU

I. ANSWERS

A. 1. ka'u keiki kāne hanauna e hana nei i ko'u hale 'aina
    2. ke keiki nīele i 'aka'aka i ka māmā kahu 'ē
    3. ka māmā kahu i lālau i ia keiki nīele
    4. ka pūpū i ho'omākaukau 'ia e Kalekona
    5. ke kanaka e ho'oku'u ana i kou ka'a

B. 1. ko'u manawa i ala ai i ke kakahiaka nui
       ka manawa o'u i ala ai ke kakahiaka nui
    2. kāna lole pupuka loa e komo ai
       ka lole pupuka loa āna e komo ai
    3. ka pūpū a Kalekona i ho'omākaukau ai
       kā Kalekona pūpū i ho'omākaukau ai
    4. kā ke kahuna pule mo'olelo e ha'i nei
       ka mo'olelo a ke kahuna pule e ha'i nei
    5. kā kona kupunahine malo i kaula'i ai ma luna o ke ahi
       ka malo a kona kupunahine i kaula'i ai ma luna o ke ahi

C. 1. 'A'ole kēia ka pūpū i ho'omākaukau 'ia e Kalekona.
    2. Na mākou i 'ai i ka pūpū a Kalekona i ho'omākaukau ai.
       Na mākou i 'ai i kā Kalekona pūpū i ho'omākaukau ai.
    3. 'Ono loa ia pūpū.
    4. Pono 'oukou e waiho i kekahi mau mea'ono na nā kānaka 'ē
       a'e.
    5. Pono 'oe e 'ai i ka mea i loa'a.
    6. 'A'ole kēia he hale 'aina.
    7. Pono 'oe e ho'omākaukau i kāu mea 'ai e 'ai ai.
       Pono 'oe e ho'omākaukau i ka mea 'ai āu e 'ai ai.
    8. Ua like loa kēlā mau ka'a hinahina.
    9. 'A'ole kēia ko Tuti ke'ena?
    10. Mai wahapa'a mai 'oe ia'u; makemake au i kekahi kalaka 'ē
        a'e e like me ko'u kalaka mua.

104

References

Burningham, Robin. 1983. *Hawaiian Word Book.* Honolulu: Bess Press.
Department of Education, State of Hawaii. 1980. *Hawaiian Language Workbook.* Honolulu.
———. 1981. *Lau Kukui, Level II Hawaiian Language Reader.* Honolulu.
Elbert, Samuel H., and Noelani K. Mahoe. 1970. *Nā Mele o Hawai'i Nei: 101 Hawaiian Songs.* Honolulu: University of Hawaii Press.
Kuykendall, Ralph S. 1953. *The Hawaiian Kingdom. Vol. 2. 1854–1874: Twenty Critical Years.* Honolulu: University of Hawaii Press.
Pukui, Mary K. 1933. *Hawaiian Folktales: Third Series.* Vassar College.
Pukui, Mary K., E. W. Haertig, and Catherine Lee. 1972. *Nana i ke Kumu.* Vols. 1 and 2. Honolulu: Hui Hanai.